DATE DUE

MIDDLE EAST NATIONS IN THE NEWS

Syria
IN THE NEWS
PAST, PRESENT, AND FUTURE

Tony Zurlo

MyReportLinks.com Books
an imprint of

 Enslow Publishers, Inc.
Box 398, 40 Industrial Road
Berkeley Heights, NJ 07922
USA

MyReportLinks.com Books, an imprint of Enslow Publishers, Inc. MyReportLinks®
is a registered trademark of Enslow Publishers, Inc.

Library of Congress Cataloging-in-Publication Data

Zurlo, Tony.
   Syria in the news : past, present, and future / Tony Zurlo.
     p. cm. — (Middle East nations in the news)
   Includes bibliographical references and index.
   ISBN 1-59845-025-5
   1. Syria—Juvenile literature.   I. Title. II. Series.
  DS93.Z87 2006
  956.91—dc22

                                  2005025654

Printed in the United States of America

10 9 8 7 6 5 4 3 2 1

To Our Readers:
Through the purchase of this book, you and your library gain access to the Report Links that specifically
back up this book.
The Publisher will provide access to the Report Links that back up this book and will keep these Report
Links up to date on **www.myreportlinks.com** for five years from the book's first publication date.
We have done our best to make sure all Internet addresses in this book were active and appropriate when
we went to press. However, the author and the Publisher have no control over, and assume no liability
for, the material available on those Internet sites or on other Web sites they may link to.
The usage of the MyReportLinks.com Books Web site is subject to the terms and conditions stated on the
Usage Policy Statement on **www.myreportlinks.com.**
A password may be required to access the Report Links that back up this book. The password is found on
the bottom of page 4 of this book.
Any comments or suggestions can be sent by e-mail to comments@myreportlinks.com or to the address
on the back cover.

Photo Credits: © 1994–29. März 2004, p. 45; © 1998:1999:2000–2005– http://www.cafe-syria.com,
p. 111; © 2001–2005 FIFA; AP Photo/Shizuo Kambayashi, p. 64; © 2002, ArabNet, p. 86; © 2002–2005
KQED & WGBH, p. 102; © 2005 Cable News Network LP, LLLP, p. 13; © 2005 Washingtonpost.Newsweek
Interactive, p. 9; © 2005 WN Network, p. 14; © Copyright 1999–2002 Syria Gate, pp. 46, 82; © Corel
Corporation, pp. 3, 30, 33, 42, 44, 54, 71, 80; AP/Wide World Photos, pp. 1, 6, 11, 98; British
Broadcasting Corporation © 2005, pp. 23, 24, 48, 94, 100, 103; Central Intelligence Agency (CIA), p. 37;
Copyright © 1996–2005 United Nations, p. 63; Copyright © 2000–2005 GlobalSecurity.org, p. 40;
Courtesy of the University of Texas Libraries, The University of Texas at Austin, pp. 16, 84; Damascus
Online, p. 52; Enslow Publishers, Inc., p. 5; Galen R. Frysinger, Sheboygan, Wisconsin, USA, p. 27; George
Baramki Azar/Saudi Aramco World/PADIA, p. 109; Ihsan Sheet/Saudi Aramco World/PADIA, pp. 3, 21,
105; International Copyright © 2005, Ministry of Tourism—Syria, p. 75; Jamie Simpson/Saudi Aramco
World/PADIA, p. 29; John Feeney/Saudi Aramco World/PADIA, p. 56; Library of Congress, pp. 39, 90, 92;
MyReportLinks.com Books, p. 4; Nik Wheeler/Saudi Aramco World/PADIA, pp. 19, 50, 59; 1996–2005,
A&E Television Networks, p. 73; Pat McDonnell/Saudi Aramco World/PADIA, p. 67; Robert Azzi/Saudi
Aramco World/PADIA, p. 112; Sana 2001, p. 114; Syria Museum, p. 68; Tor Eigeland/Saudi Aramco
World/PADIA, p. 35; U.S. State Department, p. 107; William Tracy and Khalil Abou El-Nasr/Saudi Aramco
World/PADIA, p. 77.

Cover Photo: AP/Wide World Photos

Cover Description: Syrians ride on a military truck in celebration of the return of Syrian troops from
Lebanon. By April 26, 2005, all Syrian troops had withdrawn from the neighboring country.

Contents

Merchant in Aleppo

Ruins in Palmyra

MyReportLinks.com Books
Great Books, Great Links, Great for Research!

The Internet sites featured in this book can save you hours of research time. These Internet sites—we call them **"Report Links"**—are constantly changing, but we keep them up to date on our Web site.

When you see this "Approved Web Site" logo, you will know that we are directing you to a great Internet site that will help you with your research.

Give it a try! Type http://www.myreportlinks.com into your browser, click on the series title and enter the password, then click on the book title, and scroll down to the Report Links listed for this book.

The Report Links will bring you to great source documents, photographs, and illustrations. MyReportLinks.com Books save you time, feature Report Links that are kept up to date, and make report writing easier than ever! A complete listing of the Report Links can be found on pages 116–117 at the back of the book.

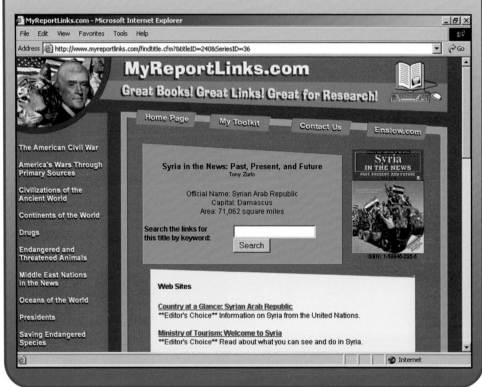

Please see "To Our Readers" on the copyright page for important information about this book, the MyReportLinks.com Web site, and the Report Links that back up this book.

Please enter **NSY1806** if asked for a password.

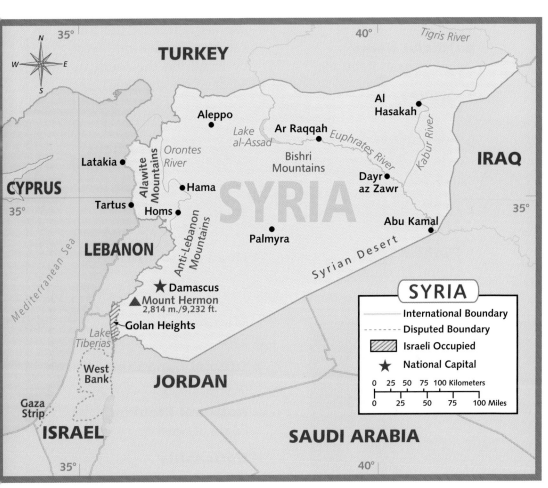

▲ A map of present-day Syria.

Flag
Red, white, and black horizontal bands of equal size, and centered in the white band, two green stars.[1]

Official Name
Syrian Arab Republic

Capital
Damascus

Population
18,448,752 (2005 estimate)

Area
71,062 square miles

Highest Point
Mount Hermon, 9,232 feet

President Bashar al-Assad

Lowest Point
Unnamed location near Lake Tiberias, 656 feet

Location
Bordered on the west by the Mediterranean Sea and Lebanon, on the southwest by Israel, on the south by Jordan, on the southeast and east by Iraq, and on the north by Turkey

Type of Government
Republic, under a military regime since March 1963

Head of State
President Bashar al-Assad

Head of Government
Prime Minister Muhammad Naji al-Utri

Monetary Unit
Syrian pound

Official Language
Arabic

National Emblem
Eagle of Saladin

Nationality
Syrian

Religion
Muslim (about 90 percent), Christian (about 10 percent), Jewish (less than 1 percent)

National Holiday
Evacuation Day (April 17)

Time Line

2250 B.C.—The earliest kingdom in the Syrian area, Ebla, is conquered by the Akkadians.

1200 B.C.—Aramaean kings rule an area called Aram (present-day Damascus).

1120 B.C.—Assyrian king Tiglath-pileser I conquers much of northern Syria.

538 B.C.—Persian king Cyrus makes Syria a province of Persia.

333 B.C.—Alexander the Great conquers the region, including Syria, for Greece.

323 B.C.—Seleucus, one of Alexander's generals, rules and names his territory Syria.

64 B.C.—Roman general Pompey conquers Syria and makes it a Roman province.

A.D. 636—*August 20:* Arab armies defeat the Byzantine forces at the Battle of Yarmuk, south of Damascus, marking the beginning of Islam's expansion.

661—*January:* Muawiya, governor of Syria, takes control of the new Arab empire with his capital in Damascus. This is the beginning of the Umayyad Dynasty.

1516—*August 24:* The Turkish Ottoman Army conquers Aleppo and soon rules over all of Syria.

1916—*May 15:* Following World War I, Great Britain and France sign the Sykes-Picot Agreement, placing Syria and Lebanon under French rule.

1946—*April 17:* The French withdraw troops from Syria. "Evacuation Day" is declared a national holiday.

1948—*May 15:* Egyptian, Jordanian, Iraqi, and Syrian troops attack Israel one day after it receives its independence.

—*March 30:* General Husni az Zaim overthrows Syria's civilian government, but the government changes hands many times from military coups over the next nine years.

1958—*February 1:* Syria joins Egypt to form the United Arab Republic (UAR), an attempt to unite Arabs together into one nation.

1961—*September 28:* Ba'ath party military leaders take over the government in Damascus and declare independence from the UAR.

1967—*June 5–10:* Syria loses the Golan Heights to Israel in the Six-Day War.

1970—*November 13:* Hafiz al-Assad takes over the government.

1971—*March 14:* Assad is sworn in as president.

1976—*April 9:* Syrian troops enter Lebanon as peacekeeping forces in the Lebanese civil war.

1982—*February:* Thousands are killed when Syrian troops enter Hama to suppress a rebellion of the Muslim Brotherhood.

1989—*October 22:* Syria and Lebanon sign the Taif Accord. Syria agrees to withdraw from Lebanon, but only after Israel withdraws its troops from southern Lebanon.

2000—*June 10:* Hafiz al-Assad dies.

—*July 10:* Assad's son, Bashar, formally assumes the presidency.

2005—*February 14:* Lebanese prime minister Rafik Hariri is murdered. Many nations suspect Syrian involvement.

—*April 26:* After international pressure, all Syrian troops are evacuated out of Lebanon.

—*October 20:* A United Nations (UN) investigation committee reports that evidence shows that Syrian and Lebanese officials were directly involved in the murder of Rafik Hariri.

Chapter 1 ▶

Current Events in Syrian News

By the end of April 2005, Syria had ended its twenty-nine year military occupation of Lebanon. The exodus followed massive anti-Syrian demonstrations by hundreds of thousands of Lebanese in the capital city of Beirut. The demonstrations were an emotional outpouring of grief for the death of former Lebanese prime minister Rafik Hariri. He

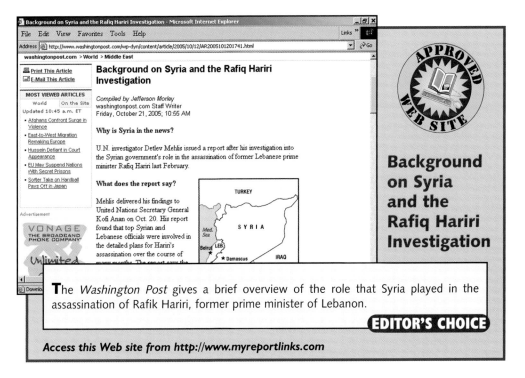

The *Washington Post* gives a brief overview of the role that Syria played in the assassination of Rafik Hariri, former prime minister of Lebanon.

EDITOR'S CHOICE

Access this Web site from http://www.myreportlinks.com

was killed on February 14, 2005, by a car bomb in Beirut. Many Lebanese accused Syrian officials of ordering his death.

American government officials also suspected that Syria was behind the killing of Hariri. White House spokesman Scott McClellan sent a clear message to Syria that the killing was "a terrible reminder that the Lebanese people must be able to pursue their aspirations and determine their own political future free from violence and intimidation and free from Syrian occupation."[1]

The United Nations (UN), France, and Germany joined United States officials in demanding that Syria withdraw so Lebanon could hold free national elections in 2005. After intense negotiations with UN representatives, Syrian president Bashar al-Assad agreed to the complete withdrawal of Syrian troops. By April 26, all of these troops had left Lebanon.

Less than six months later, a UN investigation committee reported that all available evidence suggested that top-ranking Syrian security officials, including Assad's brother and brother-in-law, were directly involved in the murder of Hariri and twenty-two others. The report also found that Syrian officials had misled and given false information to the committee. In response, the UN Security Council voted to take "further action," such as economic sanctions, against Syria if the country does not cooperate with the rest of the investigation.

▷ Palestinian Homeland

On May 15, 1948, David Ben-Gurion declared the State of Israel an independent nation within Palestine for Jewish people from around the world. Much of the Arab population resented the mass migration of Jews into their land, and five Arab nations—Syria, Lebanon, Jordan, Egypt, and

▲ Syrian soldiers ride on a military truck headed for Syria from Lebanon. All Syrian troops were withdrawn from Lebanon by April 26, 2005.

Iraq—fought unsuccessfully to stop the creation of the Jewish state. To this day, Syria considers Israel's land as rightfully belonging to the Palestinians. The Arab country resents United States foreign policy in the Middle East because it believes that this policy relies completely on America's promise to protect the independence of Israel.

Until recently, most Arab nations refused to accept Israel's right to exist. They provided support for Palestinian groups who claimed they were fighting to get their homeland back. Over the decades, Palestinian guerrillas have attacked Israelis several times a month. Usually, these attacks are carried out by one or two people at a time. Over the years, guerrillas have raided Israeli settlements, set off bombs in shopping and entertainment centers, and ambushed Israeli police and soldiers. Because civilians are often killed in the attacks, Israel and Western nations consider these attackers to be terrorists.[2]

Unlike Egypt and Jordan, Syria has refused to make peace with Israel. As a result, Syria continues to protect Palestinian guerrilla organizations within its territory.[3]

▷ Syria and United States Relations

Until 2001, Syrian relations with the United States centered on the Palestinian homeland issue. After the September 11, 2001, al-Qaeda attack on

American soil, the United States government decided to take a more active role in the Middle East. When al-Qaeda and Taliban forces were quickly defeated in Afghanistan, the United States government turned its attention to Iraq. Reasons for the American invasion of Iraq in 2003 are controversial.

Once American forces occupied Iraq, President George W. Bush declared that Syria was making it difficult for the United States to establish peace there. American authorities accused Syria of providing a hiding place for former members of Saddam Hussein's governing Ba'ath party and for militant Islamists who want to fight Americans in

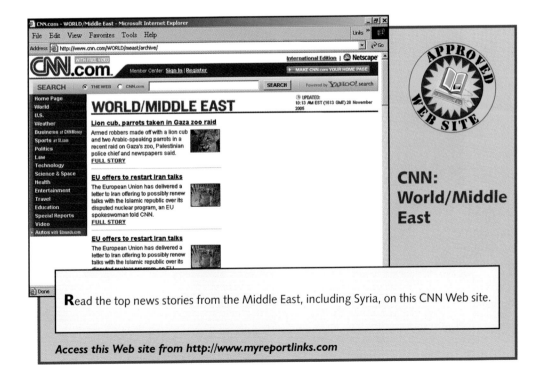

CNN: World/Middle East

Read the top news stories from the Middle East, including Syria, on this CNN Web site.

Access this Web site from http://www.myreportlinks.com

Iraq. The United States also claims that money and weapons are smuggled across the Iraqi-Syrian border to supply anti-American militants in Iraq.

In his 2005 State of the Union Address, President Bush threatened to expand penalties if Syria continued to allow "its territory, and parts of Lebanon, to be used by terrorists who seek to destroy every chance of peace in the region. . . . [W]e expect the Syrian government to end all support for terror and open the door to freedom."[4]

President Assad denies President Bush's charges, and he argues that the American invasion

Since Syrian president Bashar al-Assad took control of the Syrian government in 2000, he has introduced very little political reform in a country known for its dictatorship government. Read more about Bashar al-Assad and the latest news from the Middle East at the **Syria Daily** Web site.

EDITOR'S CHOICE

of Iraq endangers Syria's political and economic security. Assad claims that Syria tries to prevent terrorists from crossing its border into Iraq, but that it is impossible to monitor the entire 376-mile border.

Syria and WMD

Another disagreement between the United States and Syria involves the Arab nation's past desire to develop weapons of mass destruction (WMD). President Assad denies that his nation is currently developing nuclear weapons. However, he contends that as long as Israel possesses WMD (a charge that the Jewish state has never officially admitted to), then Syria has a right, if it chooses, to acquire them for self-defense.

The Center for Nonproliferation Studies (CNS) at Monterey, California, reported in 1998 that there was no evidence of a nuclear weapons program in Syria. However, Syria did have a biological weapons research program at that time, as well as stockpiles of the largest and most advanced chemical weapons in the Middle East.[5]

Chapter 2

Land and Climate

Syria is located at the northwest corner of the Mediterranean Sea. The longest distance from the Mediterranean coast to the northeastern border with Turkey and Iraq is about 515 miles. The longest north-south distance is about 460 miles. Syria's coastline is only about 120 miles long. Modern-day Syria shares borders with Turkey, Lebanon, Israel, Jordan, and Iraq.

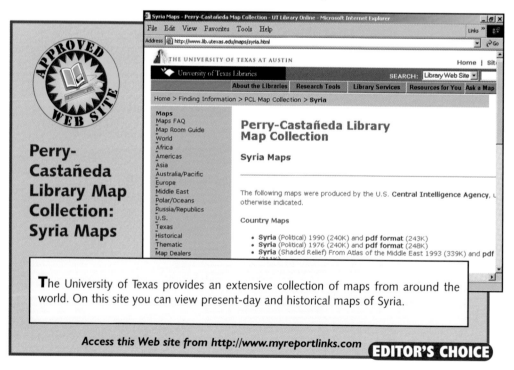

Perry-Castañeda Library Map Collection: Syria Maps

The University of Texas provides an extensive collection of maps from around the world. On this site you can view present-day and historical maps of Syria.

Access this Web site from http://www.myreportlinks.com **EDITOR'S CHOICE**

Because of its location, this region has been a major crossroads of history for more than four millennia. Until the twentieth century, the entire region that includes Syria, Lebanon, Jordan, and Israel was called Greater Syria by Western geographers.

Western Coast

From the Mediterranean Sea, Syria's coastal plains extend inland for about twenty miles. This narrow coastal region has a pleasant Mediterranean climate. The summers are dry with temperatures in the upper 80s (in degrees Fahrenheit). Most of the rainfall comes in the winter months as a result of moist ocean winds colliding with the Alawite Mountains.

Syria's two large ports are on the country's only coast, along the Mediterranean Sea. One is Tartus, near the Syria-Lebanon border, with a population about 108,000. About seventy miles to the north is Syria's main port city, Latakia. Its population is about 430,000. Latakia is located near mountains to the north and east. Annual rainfall for Latakia varies between 20 to 40 inches.

Springtime on Syria's Mediterranean coast offers spectacular views. One visitor describes a drive along the northwest coastline near Latakia: "Everything was in full bloom and beautifully green. The Acacia trees were bright yellow all along the roads. Red poppies speckled the fields, which were full of young wheat, lentils and cucumber. Everywhere there were plastic green-houses filled with tomato, cucumber, green pepper and eggplants."[1]

The Alawite Mountains are only about thirty-five miles wide. They extend north to south from Turkey for about one hundred miles. The western slopes occasionally extend to the Mediterranean coast. At an average height of about four thousand feet, the Alawite peaks are often snow covered in the winter. They absorb the humid sea winds, so some mountain locations get plenty of moisture. The mountains are covered with pine, fir, and oak trees.

▶ Orontes River Valley

The Alawite range ends short of the Lebanese border in the south. To the east, the Alawite Mountains descend rapidly to the Al Ghab depression, which is the northern part of the Great Rift Valley. It is here that the Orontes River flows northward from the Syria-Lebanon border. The Al Ghab is about forty-seven miles wide. It has more than a dozen springs and man-made underground canals that provide water for irrigation. The Al Ghab is bordered on the northeast by the Jabal az Zawiyah mountains.

The Orontes River provides water for some of Syria's major cities, such as Hama and Homs. The river also creates a fertile valley for farming. This valley is known as the Orontes River valley and is one of Syria's main farming regions despite its dry climate.

Less than 50 miles from the Lebanese border the land levels off. This low area is called the Homs Gap, named after Homs, a nearby city of 1.8 million people located on the Orontes River. Homs is less than 60 miles east of Tartus. This easy passage to the sea has made Homs an important military and trade center for almost three thousand years.

▲ *Stone mansions line the riverbanks of the Orontes River in Hama. The Orontes is unlike the other rivers of the Fertile Crescent in that it flows north, not south.*

▷ Aleppo

Syria's second largest city is Aleppo, with close to 3 million people. Located north of the Al Ghab, Aleppo is an important agricultural, education, and industrial center. Aleppo officials maintain that theirs is the oldest inhabited city in the world. (Although Damascus makes this claim as well.) They also claim to have the world's oldest covered suq, or market, at twenty-five hundred years old. There are 9 miles of streets and alleyways that make up the traditional market area. Vendors loudly call out their wares to shoppers passing by. Banners written in Arabic script are hung every-where, and many different goods, ranging from clothes to spices to fresh meat, are put up for dis-play in narrow alleyways.[2]

At an elevation of about thirteen hundred feet, Aleppo stretches out in a circle around a hill. On the top of the hill is the famous citadel, or fort. Built in 1209, the citadel has dozens of tall, stone guard towers circling the outer edge of the hill. As many as ten thousand soldiers can easily stay in the citadel. Only one invader in history has overrun the fort, according to legend: the Mongol Army, led by Tamerlane in the early fifteenth century.[3]

Aleppo has a semiarid climate. Rainfall can vary greatly, but the average annual rainfall for the city is about sixteen inches. The rain is suffi-cient to support farming in the surrounding area.

△ *The citadel sits prominently in the Aleppo skyline.*

The nearby Afrin Valley is well known for its vineyards, olive groves, and fruit orchards. Almost all of the rain in the northwest falls in late fall and winter. From May through September, temperatures often top 100°F.

Mount Hermon

In the southwest, the Anti-Lebanon Mountains serve as Syria's border with Lebanon. The highest point in the country is located in these mountains. Mount Hermon reaches nearly 9,232 feet and is snowcapped all year long.

Damascus

From the Anti-Lebanon Mountains, the Barada River flows eastward for about fifty miles. The river extends to the desert. However, the water from the Barada River creates the expansive Al Ghutah Oasis, where Damascus, Syria's capital, is located. Described by historian Philip K. Hitti, the Barada "rushes 23 miles down the slope, fans out into six main streams to irrigate a desert area and convert it into 'one of the three earthly paradises.' The 16 by 10 miles of gardens and orchards thus created, and named Ghutah, set the city like a pearl in an emerald girdle of green . . ."[4]

Since ancient times, the city of Damascus has been a center of trade. Today, Damascus is also a major industrial center. The city and its surrounding area supports a population estimated to be between 4 million and 5 million people. From Damascus, there are major highways running north about 220 miles to Aleppo; east about 150 miles to Palmyra; west about 50 miles to Beirut, Lebanon; and south about 80 miles into Jordan.

The city is bordered on the west by high fertile plains fed by underground springs. Because of the city's beauty, Damascus has many nicknames: "Bride of the Earth," "Queen of Cities," and "The Fragrant"—for the scent of jasmine that grows there. The area is well-known for its orchards of apricots, apples, cherries, plums, pears, peaches,

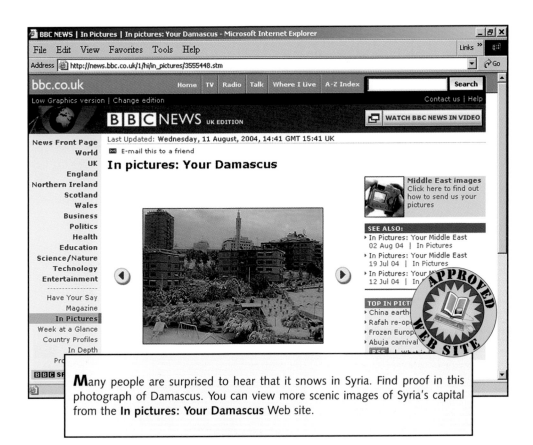

BBC NEWS | In Pictures | In pictures: Your Damascus - Microsoft Internet Explorer

File   Edit   View   Favorites   Tools   Help

Links »

Address http://news.bbc.co.uk/1/hi/in_pictures/3555448.stm

bbc.co.uk   Home   TV   Radio   Talk   Where I Live   A-Z Index   Search

Low Graphics version | Change edition   Contact us | Help

BBC NEWS UK EDITION   WATCH BBC NEWS IN VIDEO

News Front Page   Last Updated: Wednesday, 11 August, 2004, 14:41 GMT 15:41 UK
World   E-mail this to a friend
UK
England   In pictures: Your Damascus
Northern Ireland
Scotland   Middle East images
Wales   Click here to find out
Business   how to send us your
Politics   pictures
Health
Education   SEE ALSO:
Science/Nature   ▸ In Pictures: Your Middle East
Technology   02 Aug 04 | In Pictures
Entertainment   ▸ In Pictures: Your Middle East
                                                                   19 Jul 04 | In Pictures
Have Your Say   ▸ In Pictures: Your M
Magazine   12 Jul 04 | In
In Pictures   TOP IN PICT
Week at a Glance   ▸ China earth
Country Profiles   ▸ Rafah re-op
In Depth   ▸ Frozen Europ
Pr   ▸ Abuja carnival
BBC SP   RSS | Wh

Many people are surprised to hear that it snows in Syria. Find proof in this photograph of Damascus. You can view more scenic images of Syria's capital from the **In pictures: Your Damascus** Web site.

and strawberries. Damascus is said to have so impressed Muhammad, Islam's founder, that he "refused to enter the city saying that one could only enter Paradise once."[5]

Damascus averages less than 10 inches of rain a year. Most of it comes between November and March. Located on the western edge of the Syrian Desert, Damascus has extreme temperature ranges. From June through September, temperatures ranging from 100–110°F are common during the daytime. At night, the temperature drops into the 60s. The average temperature in the winter months is in the 50s, with lows that occasionally drop below freezing.

Southwestern Region

About fifty miles southwest of Damascus, Syria borders Israel at the Golan Heights. These rolling hills rise to about seventeen hundred feet above sea level. The Golan Heights were under Syrian rule until Israel occupied them in the 1967 Arab-Israeli War.

East of the Golan Heights is a small mountain range called the Jabal Druze. The highest peak

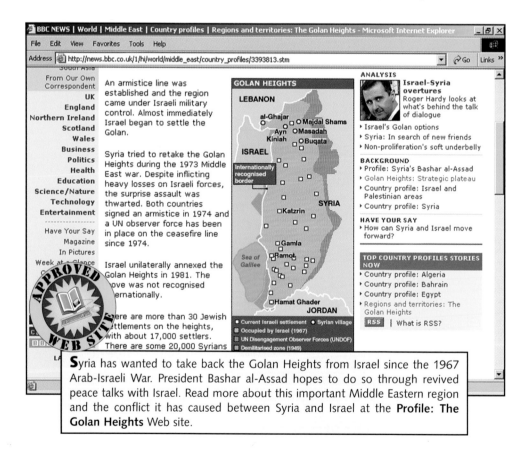

Syria has wanted to take back the Golan Heights from Israel since the 1967 Arab-Israeli War. President Bashar al-Assad hopes to do so through revived peace talks with Israel. Read more about this important Middle Eastern region and the conflict it has caused between Syria and Israel at the **Profile: The Golan Heights** Web site.

reaches about fifty-nine hundred feet. The Jabal Druze rise just north of the Yarmuk River, which forms the western part of Syria's border with Jordan, and eventually drop about two thousand feet to the Hawran Plateau, south of Damascus. The Hawran is filled with volcanic rock and has no trees. However, the plateau gets enough rainfall to support the farming of wheat, barley, and beets.

▶ Central Region

Central Syria begins east of the Jabal az Zawiyah mountains. In the far northern portion, mountain valleys are an important land feature. Most of the land receives enough water to support agriculture. The remaining portion of central Syria is made up of extensive semiarid plains that stretch eastward to the Euphrates River. Cereal crops such as wheat, barley, and maize are grown in some parts of this area. The major city on the Euphrates River is Ar Raqqah, with about 120,000 people. This provincial capital is important because of nearby oil fields and the Euphrates Dam project.

East and south of the Jabal az Zawiyah mountains, the land turns rapidly into a plateau of steppe and desert. This semiarid landscape extends all the way into Iraq and Jordan. Two thousand years ago, caravans crossed this steppe and desert between Damascus, Syria, and Baghdad, Iraq. The most common vegetation is dwarf shrub sagebrush. Reeds and small trees survive close to water sources.

There are a few mammals living in the steppe region. These include wolves, sand foxes, wild-cats, gazelles, and wild boars. The steppe also includes the middle third of the Euphrates River, which is an important migration route for many types of birds. Flamingos, falcons, pygmy cor-morants, marbled teals, and turtledoves are just a few of the birds that are found along the Euphrates and surrounding land.

Euphrates River

The north-central and eastern areas of Syria are dominated by the Euphrates River. From the mountains of Turkey, the Euphrates winds south-east for 423 miles through Syria into Iraq. The river supplies 80 percent of Syria's water resources. Two major rivers, the Khabur and the Balikh, empty into the east bank of the Euphrates. The plant life along the river consists mostly of poplar, tamarix, and willow trees, in addition to reed grass and cattails.

In 1973, the Euphrates Dam (also known as the Tabaqah Dam), about two hundred feet high and almost three miles long, was completed north of the city of Ar Raqqah. The city of Al Thawra was created just to take care of the dam and the lake formed by the dam, Lake Assad. The power plant

The Euphrates is the longest river in Syria. It is a very shallow river, making navigation by boat near impossible. However, the Euphrates has been valuable in irrigating the land. Take a virtual tour of Syria through images at this **Syria** Web site.

built at the lake began providing hydroelectric power to villages throughout the north-central and northeastern region in 1977. The lake, which is 50 miles long and 5 miles wide, and the dam have become major sources for irrigation projects.

▷ Eastern Region

The far northeastern part of Syria is called Al Jazirah, or island. This small section of rolling plateau extends eastward from the Euphrates River for about 175 miles to the western shores of the Tigris River. It is populated by a mixture of ethnic groups, including a large number of Kurds and Assyrians. The people work mostly as farmers. They get most of their water from the 200 mile-long Khabur River. In recent decades, the Syrians have found gas and oil reserves in the east, which are an important part of the national income.

The Khabur joins the Euphrates near Dayr az Zawar, which is a three-hour bus ride southeast of Ar Raqqah. Between May and November, Dayr az Zawar receives almost no rain at all. From April through October, high daytime temperatures of over 100°F are normal. In the winter months, freezing temperatures are common. About one hundred miles to the southeast is the town of Abu Kamal, on the Iraqi border. Beyond the Euphrates valley, the landscape is all desert and arid, rocky hills.

Khamsin

During April and May and again at the end of summer in September and October, Syria is hit with a hot, dusty wind called khamsin. These winds blow in from the Arabian peninsula located to the south. These winds can blow for three or four days, and temperatures can often top 120°F.

Desert Land

Syrians use the term *badiyah*, or Bedouin-land, for the long desert that stretches between Al Jazirah south and east to the borders of Jordan and Iraq.

The term refers to the nomadic people who spend part of each year grazing sheep and/or camels there.[6]

This area is part of the Syrian Desert, where almost all the land is covered with sand. There is no vegetation. This desert covers more than 20 percent of Syria's land area. Sections often have local names, such as the Hamad Desert in the south-central part of Syria and the Homs Desert north and east of Homs.

Desert covers more than 20 percent of Syria's land.

Palmyra is located in the Syrian Desert. It was once the capital of Syria and an important political and economic center on the Silk Route, connecting the Orient and Europe. Palmyra thrived until A.D. 272, when the Roman Army destroyed it. Today, visitors may tour the beautiful ruins.

The major city in the Syrian Desert is Palmyra. Its name means city of palms, after the trees that grow there on a huge oasis. Centrally located about 95 miles east of the Orontes River and 124 miles west of the Euphrates River, Palmyra's climate is hot and dry. Summer temperatures regularly top 110°F. Most of the region receives less than 6 inches of rain annually.

In the nearby mountains, the Afqa Springs have been used for more than three millennia for mineral water baths. Although this is all desert, the land consists of more than just sand. Much of it is rolling plains between 1,000 to 1,600 feet high, filled with rock and gravel.

▷ Land of Religions

Because of Syria's central location, missionaries and armies carrying religious messages crossed through Syria for thousands of years. The Jews and Christians came from Palestine in the south. The Arabs spread across the desert from the southeast. Romans and Greeks brought their ideas from the west across the Mediterranean. And in later centuries, Europeans sought to replant the ideas of Christianity in the Middle East by traveling through Syria.

Religion

The three major religions of the Western world—Judaism, Christianity, and Islam—trace their heritage to the Middle East. According to the biblical story, the prophet Abraham had no children, so his wife, Sarah, agreed to let him take a second wife. Abraham married Hagar, Sarah's Egyptian maid. They had a son named Ishmael. Arabs consider Ishmael to be the first Arab. When Abraham and Sarah were past ninety years old, they had Isaac, the ancestor of the Jewish people.

▷ Muhammad and Islam

The efforts of one man changed the lives of the people dramatically. He was an Arab trader named Muhammad who lived in Mecca on the Arabian peninsula.

The Arab people included tribes of Bedouin nomads and settled families in towns. Most of them lived on the Arabian peninsula, but Arabs also could be found in areas of modern-day Syria, Lebanon, Jordan, Iraq, and Palestine.

Before Muhammad, many Arabs worshiped multiple gods. They shared the common belief that they were descendents of Abraham. Mecca was their holy city. The religious shrine in Mecca, called the Kaaba, housed statues that represented

▲ *Mecca, Saudi Arabia, is the most holy city in Islam. Muslims must face Mecca when they pray. Mihrabs, or niches, are carved into mosques to show worshippers where they must face. The imam stands in front of the mosque's mihrab when leading prayers.*

the several hundred gods. Muhammad believed that Arabs would never be a strong, unified people as long as they believed in many gods. He taught that there was only one true God. He preached that if Arabs would abandon their beliefs in many gods and worship the one true God, they would be rewarded with unity and strength. Mecca's leading families feared Muhammad's power, so they planned to attack him. But in 622, Muhammad and his followers escaped and settled 200 miles to the northwest in Medina. This migration to Medina is called the hijra in Arabic. The year 622 is the most important date in Islamic history.

In Medina, Muhammad exercised his political skills. He brought together various ethnic and religious groups so they would live peacefully. At the same time, Muhammad ruled his community of Muslims, called umma, with absolute authority.

▷ Spread of Islam

During the next eight years, Muhammad's soldiers battled neighboring Arab tribes. Often the tribes converted to Islam. Finally, in 630, Muhammad had enough military strength to march on Mecca. The authorities there surrendered peacefully. Muhammad died in 632 before his armies had time to move into southern Syria. However, he had established a new religion, Islam, that soon dominated the entire Middle East

▲ *Muslims believe that the Qur'an is the direct word of God, told to Muhammad through the angel Gabriel. The Qur'an provides guidelines for how Muslims should live their lives.*

and North Africa. He left behind a holy book, the Qur'an, to guide people's daily lives. And his political skills inspired Arabs to unify under a single government.[1]

Within four years after Muhammad's death, Muslim troops had overpowered the Christian Byzantine forces at the Yarmuk River in Damascus. By 661 most of modern-day Syria was under Muslim rule. The Arabs were led by the

Umayyad family, who established their capital in Damascus.

To strengthen his power, the Muslim caliph (ruler), Amir Muawiya, maintained the existing system of government used by the Byzantines. Muawiya also made changes that helped the Muslim empire keep its Arab base. For one, he made Arabic the official language of the government. In addition, he ordered all coins be stamped only with Arabic and Arab symbols.[2]

Some Arabs tried to live apart from the native population. Arab tribes who had converted to Islam were given stipends. Eventually, many Arab army men settled in Syrian cities and worked in trade and businesses. Over the centuries, Arab men and women intermarried with locals.

The caliphs preserved Islam and the Arabic language, and Damascus became a center for Islamic culture. The religion spread over the next several centuries, and most of the native people became Muslims. Syrians joined the army in large numbers. In less than one century, the Muslim Army conquered lands from Persia (modern-day Iran) and India, across North Africa, all the way north to Spain.

Sunnis

After the third caliph, Uthman, was assassinated in 656, a dispute broke out over who should be

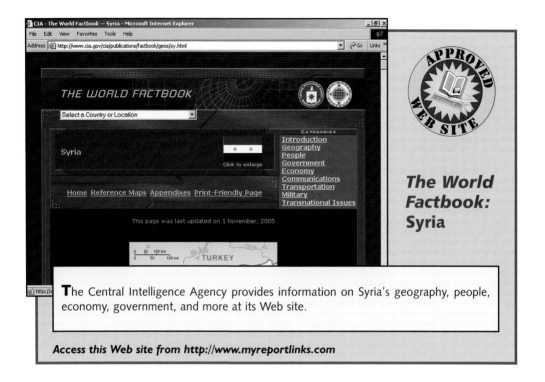

The Central Intelligence Agency provides information on Syria's geography, people, economy, government, and more at its Web site.

Access this Web site from http://www.myreportlinks.com

the next leader of the Muslims. Ali, Muhammad's cousin and son-in-law, claimed the position. He established his capital in southern Iraq. However, Muawiya, governor of Syria and Uthman's cousin, challenged Ali. The struggle ended five years later when Ali was murdered.

Muawiya represented the majority of Muslims, now called the Sunnis. They believe that the caliph should be selected by representatives of the Muslim community. Sunnis argue that God instructed Muhammad to tell his followers, "If ye love Allah, follow me [Muhammad]; Allah will love you and forgive you your sins. Allah is Forgiving, Merciful."[3] This verse, Sunnis believe, refers to Muhammad's personal behavior. Sunni scholars have organized Muhammad's sayings and stories about his life into several volumes called the Sunnah.

Shi'ites

The Shi'ites, or Party of Ali, emerged as the major opponents to Sunni dominance. They believed that only a relative of Muhammad should become caliph. However, after Ali was murdered, his sons were killed while opposing Muawiya. As a result, the Shi'ites had to live separately as a minority community. Today, Shi'ites make up about 15 percent of the Syrian population.

Shi'ites also differ in their beliefs about the position of the imam. The Sunnis believe that the imam is simply a man well educated in Islam. He often has a leadership position at a mosque where he leads group prayer and can act as a religious counselor. For Shi'ites, however, there is only one imam. The Shi'ites believe this imam can make no mistakes when offering religious opinions. The largest group of Shi'ite Muslims is called the Twelvers because they believe that there were twelve imams, beginning with Ali. The last imam, however, disappeared around 874. Shi'ites believe that he went into hiding, and they expect him to return someday and reign over a peaceful kingdom.

▷ Alawis

People who call themselves Alawis make up the largest religious minority group in Syria. Alawi means followers of Ali, and they claim to be Shi'ites. Many beliefs of the Alawi religion are secret. However, it is known that Alawis read the Qur'an and accept some of the teachings of Islam, but they also believe ideas from Christianity and other religions. Sunni and Shi'ite Muslims contend that Alawis are not really Muslims because they do not follow the sharia, or laws of the Qur'an. Sunnis and Shi'ites condemn Alawis for drinking wine and observing Christian religious holidays such as Christmas and Easter, among other practices.

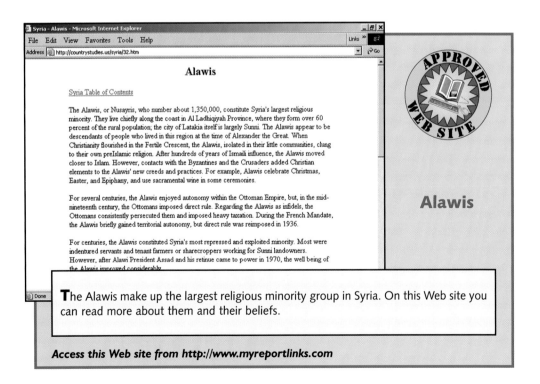

The Alawis make up the largest religious minority group in Syria. On this Web site you can read more about them and their beliefs.

Access this Web site from http://www.myreportlinks.com

Alawis in Syria number close to 2 million people. Most live in the northwest in rural areas near the city of Latakia and in the Alawite Mountains. For centuries, they have been treated poorly by different conquering empires.

After World War I, many Alawis were poor peasants. These Alawis often worked as sharecroppers and as indentured servants to Sunni Muslims. Many Alawis joined the army to escape their poor conditions. Many eventually gained prominent positions within the Syrian Army, and military factions began to compete to control the country. Between 1955 and 1970, Alawis in the military led by Hafiz al-Assad became powerful

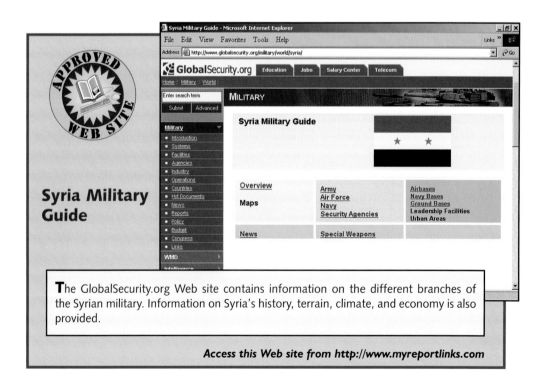

The GlobalSecurity.org Web site contains information on the different branches of the Syrian military. Information on Syria's history, terrain, climate, and economy is also provided.

Access this Web site from http://www.myreportlinks.com

enough to take over the government. Since that time most of the top military and government leaders have been Alawis.

Basic Teachings of Islam

Muslims believe there is one all-powerful and eternal God who created the universe. God has sent great men to earth to spread his message. Adam was the first of these great prophets. Among the most notable of the many others are Noah, Abraham, Ishmael, Moses, John the Baptist, Jesus, and Muhammad.

The last prophet, Muhammad, founded Islam. In Arabic, Islam means total surrender to Allah's will. Therefore, people must obey Allah's words. Muslims believe that Allah sent the archangel Gabriel to convey these words, which are recorded in the Qur'an.

Muhammad taught that humans have a free will to choose how they live. He warned, however, that there will be a judgment day when Allah will reward or punish humans for eternity in heaven or hell.

Five Pillars of Islam

Muslims follow the basic fundamentals of faith called the Five Pillars. These are the creed, prayer, almsgiving, fasting, and pilgrimage.

The first pillar is the creed, or *shahada*. Whenever praying, Muslims must declare, preferably in

Arabic, the following: "There is no god but the God (Allah) and Muhammad is the messenger of God."[4] This must be done publicly at least once in a Muslim's lifetime, but most do it daily.

Prayer, or *salah,* is the second pillar. Muslims are required to pray five times a day: at dawn, noon, afternoon, sunset, and after sunset. Each time, participants prepare themselves by cleansing their feet, arms, and face. Although group prayer is preferred, prayer can be offered anywhere as long as the participant faces Mecca. On Fridays at noon, Muslim men gather for group prayer at a

▲ A Muslim man kneels to pray at the Shrine of Ibn-Arabi, one of the many sacred sites in Damascus.

mosque. An imam leads group prayers. Women can participate but only from a segregated part of the mosque.

Almsgiving, the third pillar of Islam, is called *zakat*. In Arabic, the word means to purify the heart and soul by helping those less fortunate. Islam requires Muslims who can afford it to give 2.5 percent of their wealth annually to charity.

The fourth pillar is fasting between dawn and sunset during the month of Ramadan. Called *sawm,* this pillar honors the month that Muhammad received Allah's words from the archangel Gabriel. By fasting for the entire month, believers are reminded that being a good Muslim requires self-discipline.

The fifth pillar is the pilgrimage to Mecca, Saudi Arabia, called the *hajj.* All Muslims who are financially and physically able must visit the holy city of Mecca once in their lifetime. The purpose of the hajj is to offer complete humility and surrender to Allah's will. Muslims from all nations, races, and social classes gather in one place to worship together.

Teachings of the Qur'an

Faith in Allah, the one God, is the focus of Islam. But the Qur'an also teaches that people must do good deeds to be saved. The reward for those who combine belief and action is eternal life in heaven.

This man prepares bread during Ramadan. At this time, Muslims may not eat, drink, smoke, or engage in sexual intercourse between dawn and sunset.

▶ Influence of Islam on the State

The Syrian government is secular, meaning that it is not religious, and Syria has a reputation for being one of the more moderate Arab nations. However, Islam does play a part in the government. For instance, the Syrian constitution requires the nation's president to be Muslim. It also states that the sharia is a major source for laws. At the same time, the constitution says nothing about Islam being the state religion, and the constitution guarantees freedom of worship.

The legal system reflects the mixture of religious cultures that have existed in Syria for more than fifteen centuries. There are civil and criminal courts that deal with serious legal issues that are not specifically related to Islam. However, religion heavily influences the laws that govern courts for personal and family matters.

Religion is not considered an important part of the curriculum; however, it is a required course for all students through high school. Students can learn about Islam or Christianity. According to scholar Joshua M. Landis of the University of Oklahoma, "The twelfth grade text explains that Islam is responsible for making the Arabs great. 'The revelation of Islamic principles transformed the Arabs into a unified community (*umma*) possessing a high human civilization which it spread to all people.'" The text also explains that Islam unified the Arab tribes and guided them to a high level of moral living.[5]

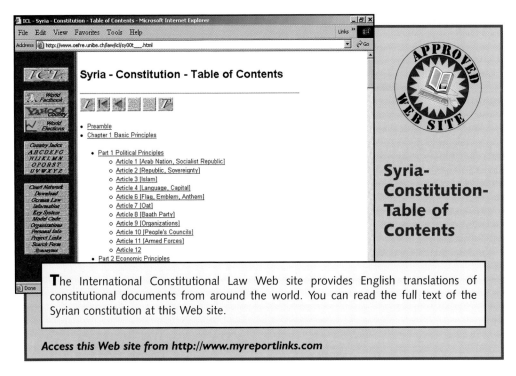

The International Constitutional Law Web site provides English translations of constitutional documents from around the world. You can read the full text of the Syrian constitution at this Web site.

Access this Web site from http://www.myreportlinks.com

Since the early 1980s, the Syrian government has recommended topics for sermons in the mosques. If an imam promotes ideas that seem to threaten the current political regime, then the government might arrest the imam.

▷ Militant Islam

Militant conservative Muslim groups in Syria have pointed to the deteriorating economy as proof that the government has abandoned Islamic teachings. A conservative Muslim organization called the Muslim Brotherhood demanded that the Syrian government abandon secular rule and adopt strict sharia. In 1958, the Syrian government had banned the group from politics. In June 1980, the

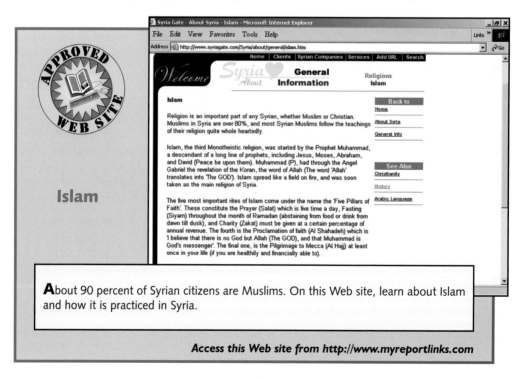

About 90 percent of Syrian citizens are Muslims. On this Web site, learn about Islam and how it is practiced in Syria.

Access this Web site from http://www.myreportlinks.com

Brotherhood failed in an assassination attempt on Syrian president Hafiz al-Assad. The government immediately passed a law making membership in the Brotherhood punishable by death. Tensions between the government and the Brotherhood soon exploded. In 1982, Assad sent the army to attack rioters in Hama.[6] Syrian troops killed as many as ten thousand people within a few weeks. This put an end to the Muslim Brotherhood in Syria.

▷ Syria and the World of Islam

Syria's location puts it in the center of the Muslim world. Lebanon, with a slight Muslim majority, has a large Christian minority. The rest of the Middle Eastern and North African nations have large Muslim majorities. Only Israel, which borders Syria to the south, is without a Muslim majority.

Relations with the Muslim nations are normally friendly, partly because they share a common religion. However, instability in the region worries Syrian authorities. If Shi'ites come into power in Iraq, they could form an alliance with the Shi'ite dominated government of Iran. Together these Shi'ite nations could assist the enemies of the Ba'ath government in Syria.

Islam, in addition to political and trade relations, connects Syria to countries around the world. In 1969, Syria was one of the founding members of the Organization of the Islamic

The BBC provides all the latest news from the Middle East, including Syria.

Access this Web site from http://www.myreportlinks.com

Conference (OIC), which now has fifty-seven members. The organization works toward strengthening ties between member nations, increased cooperation between members and nonmembers, and the return of territory to Palestinians.

Chapter 4

Syrian Culture

Nearly 90 percent of Syria's 18 million people are Arab. Another 9 percent are Kurds, who live mostly in the northeast. In addition, there are small groups of Armenians, Turkomans, and other ethnic groups living mostly in the north and in some of the larger cities.

About 10 percent of Syrians practice religions other than Islam. The overwhelming Muslim majority follows Islamic teachings as a guide for daily living. However, today almost 55 percent of Syrians are under nineteen years old. And these Syrians are mixing modern ideas from the West with their traditional customs.

▶ Changing Society

Prior to Syria's independence from French rule, the most important people in society were religious leaders and wealthy landowners. However, the social structure in Syria began to change in the 1960s. The ruling Ba'ath party encouraged the rise of a bureaucratic middle class that profited from several industries, including land reform, import-export businesses, and construction. The

Syria's population is very young. Almost 55 percent of Syrians are under nineteen years old, and the country's median age is just over twenty years old. The median age in the United States is just over thirty-six years old.

top-level government officials and their family members knew ahead of time about future government projects. Therefore, they were granted contracts to start up businesses that would return great profits to them in the future.[1] Many of these companies were involved in building and construction of roads, dams, and housing; extracting and refining oil; processing food; and importing and exporting consumer goods.

In addition to these government officials, this new Syrian middle class included those in society with higher education, such as teachers, lawyers, technicians, and doctors. Many traditional Sunni leaders lost their authority. Some of them married into the new bureaucratic class, hoping to maintain some influence. Others made business deals with members of the new class.

▷ Urban Syria

The growth of the urban population in Syria has been rapid since the country's independence from France. Today, more than 50 percent of Syrians live in cities. As new groups of people migrate to urban areas, they build on the outside edge of the older sections. This adding-on process over the last century has created separate city sections.

The oldest neighborhoods usually contain the traditional markets and shops for craftsmen and artisans. When the Greeks and Romans ruled, they

http://www.damascus-online.com/Photos/sham/DSCN2745.jpg - Microsoft Internet Explorer

File   Edit   View   Favorites   Tools   Help   Links »

Address   http://www.damascus-online.com/Photos/sham/DSCN2745.jpg   Go

Much of Syria is rural, however, the country's urban areas have been expanding rapidly. Shown here is modern Damascus. Find other photos and historical information on the **Damascus Online: Everything Syrian** Web site.

EDITOR'S CHOICE

built houses and shops that reflected their cultures. Each new group usually practiced a different religion, so they built their own places of worship.

Traditionally, the typical city resident lives with his or her extended family in the Muslim quarter, with close relatives nearby. In older sections of Syrian cities, many of the traditional houses are two- to five-story stone buildings with solid walls that border streets. Rooms were built to face inward, to a central, open courtyard where cooking, washing, and socializing take place. Today in large cities, mixed neighborhoods are common. People often live in apartments. Except for the extremely rich, different economic classes are mixed together in the traditional Muslim quarters.

Since the early twentieth century, more modern neighborhoods have risen on the outskirts of old cities. These suburban communities house new industries and their employees. Most of them are near Damascus, Aleppo, and Latakia.

Rural Life

Most of the rural population in Syria are peasants living in small villages. They rely on irrigation or irregular rainfall to grow crops. Traditionally, peasants worked land owned by a landowner who lived in a nearby city. Since land reform laws in the 1960s, more peasants own their land. However, many still depend on loans to keep up their small farms.

Usually the men plant, harvest, and process the crops. The women do housework, care for children, and tend to animals. However, today many women work in the fields as well, weeding and harvesting. Boys are often left in school so they can finish their secondary education. Girls, on the other hand, are often pulled out of school as soon as possible to work.

To make extra money, teenage girls often work at more than one location. One study describes a typical village girl's yearly work schedule: She tends sheep from December through February and helps with milking and processing the milk into yogurt. From March through May, she helps her family make mud blocks for their home, make cheese, and harvest crops. Then between June and August, she commutes to a town over 80 miles away to harvest potatoes, sugar beets, onions, and vegetables for wages. She returns home each day to continue her duties at home. In September she commutes to a village nearly 56 miles away to harvest cotton from dawn to dusk.[2]

△ A Syrian woman retrieves water from a well in Aleppo.

Family

Many rural and urban Syrians prefer living in an extended family environment, although this is changing. This family environment can include an older couple, their married sons and their families, unmarried children of the older couple, and even relatives from the male side of the family. However, it is more typical for only six or seven people from three generations to live together.

Syrian Cuisine

Meals are family affairs. One of the main foods is pita bread, or flat bread. It is eaten at every meal. Syrians use bread to pick up pieces of food to eat. For breakfast, Syrians often eat tomato and fava bean salad, cheese, olives, and melon slices.

The most common meats for lunch and dinner are roasted chicken and lamb. Eggplant and rice are also popular at these meals. The food is usually flavored with garlic, onions, red peppers, paprika, and/or lemon juice. Sauces are used for food dip. One of these is called tahini, a paste made from crushed sesame seeds. Another popular dip is called hummus, which is chickpea paste with spices and olive oil.

After dinner, many families stroll along city streets to socialize. Some people sit in cafés and sip tea, coffee, or fruit drinks. *Sous* is another favorite drink. It is brown in color and tastes like black licorice. Syrians often snack on roasted watermelon and pumpkin seeds, chestnuts, and grape leaves stuffed with vegetables and meat. Another favorite snack is *shwarma*. These are small chunks of roasted chicken, wrapped inside pita bread. For flavoring, the shwarma can include garlic mayonnaise, yogurt, and sour pickle slices.

▷ Marriage and the Family

Marrying and raising a family is considered a person's duty in Syria. In the past, Syrian men

▲ Stuffed vegetables are also a part of the Syrian diet. Shown here are stuffed zucchini, eggplant, green peppers, and tomatoes.

married in their early twenties and women in their mid- to late- teens. Today, except in rural areas, Syrians prefer to finish their education and work for a few years first. Most of these single adults live at home with their parents until they get married. Today, especially in urban areas, most Syrians marry in their mid- to late- twenties.

Arranged marriages are still common. Marriage is seen as a contract between families, not just between two people. Therefore, elder family members have a strong voice in choosing mates for their children. Syrian custom encourages marriage between cousins. Christian Syrians have broken with this tradition.

In urban areas, arranged marriages are less popular. However, parents usually have to approve of their children's choices for spouses. The groom's family usually offers a dowry, consisting of several years' income, to the bride's family. This money is often paid only if the marriage ends in divorce.

Divorce

Divorce for Muslims follows the rules of the Qur'an. These rules are also spelled out in the laws called personal status codes. Either spouse can go to a sharia court and ask for divorce. The husband has another option, though. He can simply declare to his wife on three separate occasions that he divorces her. Still, divorce is not common in Syria. Only about 7 percent of marriages end in divorce.

▷ Women in Society

In Syria, men still consider women weaker and in need of protection. The Qur'an says that men are stronger and therefore they are responsible for the economic welfare of women. Since men must support women, good women are those who obey men.[3]

Most husbands treat their wives fairly; however, wife abuse is a growing concern among human rights activists in Syria. It is difficult to bring a case of spousal abuse to court. It is easier for women to divorce husbands who fail to provide adequate economic support. The sharia requires a husband to provide all of his wife's physical needs, from clothes and food to housing and medicine.[4]

Except for in the home, women traditionally live separate lives from men. Muslim women who go out are expected to wear long, loose-fitting dresses that cover the entire body, although some women do not. In many parts of Syria, a woman also covers her hair and most of her face. In rural Syria, a Muslim woman normally covers her head with a *hijab,* or scarf. Some still cover their hair and body with a longer wraparound called a chador.

In Syrian cities, many women wear loose-fitting Western suits and dresses. Some Muslim

This elderly Syrian woman wears a hijab and chador.

women do not even wear the hijab. For instance, younger non-Muslim women and many Muslim teenagers sometimes appear in public in jeans and casual blouses. Even in this more open environment, though, men and women are still segregated, except for official business.

Syria's personal status laws reinforce the dominance of males in society. Although polygamy is discouraged, Syrian laws follow the Qur'an and permit men to marry up to four wives. (However, a recent law now requires the consent of the wife before her husband can take a second wife.) In addition, a woman must get the official consent of a male guardian before marrying. Otherwise, her marriage can be annulled.

▶ Children

A Syrian wife's main duty is to care for and train her children. Children are expected to obey their parents without questioning them. However, young people are becoming more independent. Some believe that exposure to foreign cultures through movies, music, and television has played a part in this change.[5]

Syrians today are much better educated than any previous generation. The law requires all children to attend elementary and intermediate secondary school. For students who qualify to continue their education, public education is free of charge.

▷ Education

The Syrian government tries to control what young people learn about the world in the country's government-controlled public schools. The Ministry of Education sets the curricula for all levels. Since 1967, Syria has promoted Arab cultural identity in its public schools. Elementary school students study Arab culture and Islam, geography, math, Arabic, history, and literature. After completing the sixth grade, students receive a certificate that allows them to apply for acceptance to intermediate, or lower, secondary school for grades seven through nine.

In intermediate secondary school, students continue studying the major fields introduced in elementary school. At the end of three years, the intermediate school students take an examination called the Intermediate Level Diploma (ILD). This exam determines which type of upper-level secondary school a student may attend. There is the college track and the technical track. The technical track provides students with technical training so that they can enter the job market right after their secondary education. Many students do not pursue this upper level of education. In 2001, when only elementary education was required, only 45 percent of the eligible girls attended either secondary level. The majority stayed at home and worked for their parents.

About one third of those in intermediate schools go on to attend upper secondary schools. In the 1990s, 70 percent of these students selected the technical track. For their three-year program, they select one of several fields: industrial (chosen by 50 percent of the students), commercial (20 percent), agricultural (fewer than 10 percent), or "female" courses such as home economics and nursing.[6] Then they take an exam called the Technical Baccalaureate. High scores enable students to continue their studies at the Institute of Technical Education.

Students in the general track in upper secondary school choose either the literary or scientific track. After three years of study, these students take the Baccalaureate Secondary School Leaving Certificate exam, which will determine if they are qualified to go on to a university for bachelor degree programs.

There are four major universities: Damascus University, Tishreen University in Latakia, the University of Aleppo, and Al Ba'ath University in Homs. There are also new university level programs being introduced by the United Nations that are being taught over the Internet.

▷ Technology in Education

Syria's President Bashar al-Assad has promoted the expansion of information technology education

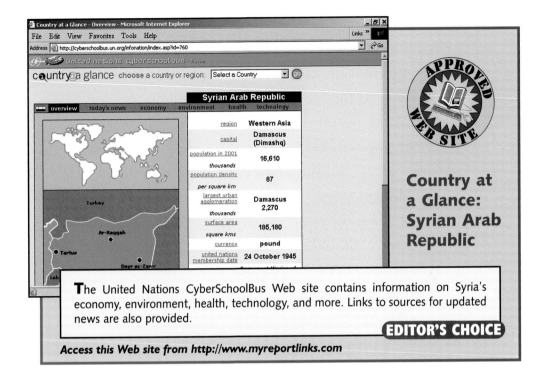

The United Nations CyberSchoolBus Web site contains information on Syria's economy, environment, health, technology, and more. Links to sources for updated news are also provided.

EDITOR'S CHOICE

Access this Web site from http://www.myreportlinks.com

in the schools. As a former president of Syria's Computer Society (SCS), Assad has made computer literacy and Internet access a major goal of the Ministry of Education.

▷ Recreation and Entertainment

With satellite television, Syrian young people follow popular culture from around the country and the world. They follow the careers of famous athletes, singers, and actors.

Syrian males are often big soccer fans. Soccer is called football in Syria. From an early age, they play soccer in the streets, on playgrounds, and at school. Teams that represent schools and towns play in competition all year. The Syrian football federation selects national teams to compete for the World Cup competition. Syrians also send teams to compete in the Asian football cup and the World Youth Cup tournaments every year. Other popular sports in Syria include basketball, badminton, and running events.

Besides sports, a favorite pastime for Syrians is listening to music. Traditional Arab music is popular with older Syrians. But Syrians under twenty-five listen to popular music from around the world. Performers from the Middle East

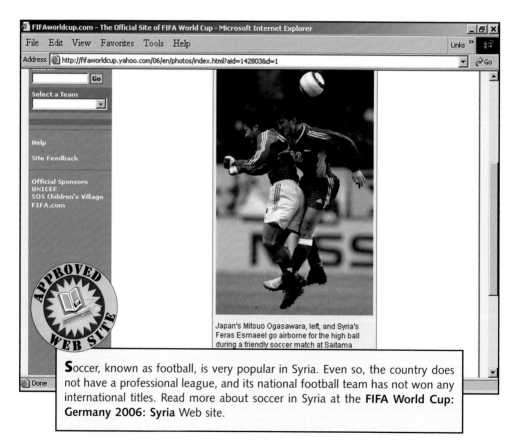

Japan's Mitsuo Ogasawara, left, and Syria's Feras Esmaeel go airborne for the high ball during a friendly soccer match at Saitama

Soccer, known as football, is very popular in Syria. Even so, the country does not have a professional league, and its national football team has not won any international titles. Read more about soccer in Syria at the **FIFA World Cup: Germany 2006: Syria** Web site.

and North Africa are the most popular. Egyptian Amr Diab and Iraqi Kazem Al Saher are two of the best known. Popular Syrian singers include Asala Nasri, George Wassouf, Ruwaida Attieh, and Mayada Al Hinawi.

Watching television is an everyday activity as well. The government owns and operates the only three networks in Syria, but Syrians get other programs by satellite. Arabic language programs are the most popular.

Like people around the world, Syrians enjoy comedies and dramas, sports, and popular movies. One of the most popular programs every year is the *Arab Idol* show, modeled after the *American Idol* series. Large screens are placed in city streets so the people can watch. Posters and advertisements urge people to cast their vote for the Syrian contestant.

Even though Western cultures have influenced Syrian artistic tastes, Syrian and Arab writers and artists have created their own distinctive styles influenced by local tastes and customs. Most Syrians consider the Qur'an as the greatest example of poetic writing. But today, there are dozens of popular authors, from novelists Nihad Sirees and Hani al-Dhahabi to poets Nizar Qabbani and Nazih Abu Afash.

Early History

Before the twentieth century, Greater Syria was a cultural crossroads. Land routes stretched from southern Europe, along the Mediterranean coast, and across central Asia along the Silk Road all the way to Xi'an, the capital of ancient China. The Mediterranean trade routes connected Syria with Egypt to the south and the African kingdoms to the southwest.

▷ Ancient Syria

Because of this trade, some of the world's earliest cities emerged in this area. Both Aleppo and Damascus claim to be the world's longest inhabited city, dating back at to least 2300 B.C. In the nearby river valleys, people grew wheat and other grains. On the steppes, nomadic tribes grazed their sheep, goats, and camels. Migrations of different groups of people crossed into modern-day Syria and Lebanon.

One of the earliest kingdoms was Ebla, located just a few miles south of Aleppo. Around 2250 B.C., Ebla was overrun by the Akkadian kingdom

▲ Damascus still has its ancient quarter, containing the Temple of Jupiter (foreground) and the Via Recta, or the "Street Called Straight."

from the southeast. Soon afterwards, the Canaanites settled on the coastlines of modern-day Israel, Lebanon, and Syria. This group of people developed prosperous city-states such as Byblos, Tyre, and Sidon. Their descendants, called the Phoenicians, developed one of the world's earliest writing systems to use as an alphabet. The Hebrew, Arabic, Greek, and Latin alphabets derive their beginnings from the Phoenicians.

Another ethnic group that influenced the region were the Aramaeans. In the twelfth century B.C., they established the kingdom of Aram as

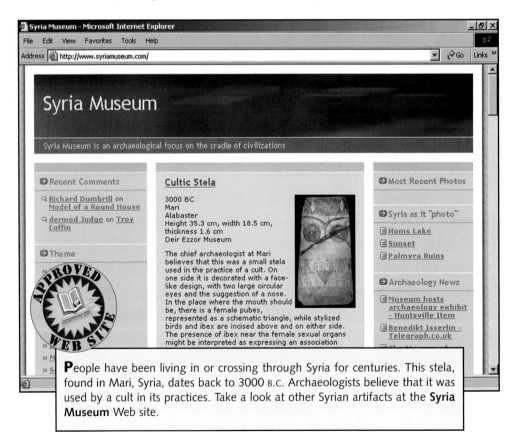

People have been living in or crossing through Syria for centuries. This stela, found in Mari, Syria, dates back to 3000 B.C. Archaeologists believe that it was used by a cult in its practices. Take a look at other Syrian artifacts at the **Syria Museum** Web site.

well as many other smaller kingdoms throughout the interior of Syria. The capital of one of these kingdoms was Damascus, which became a wealthy city. By the eighth century, the Aramaean language, called Aramaic, was the major language throughout the region. It was commonly spoken by residents for another thousand years.

Egypt ruled over this region for about two centuries, but in the eighth century B.C., the Egyptians were overtaken by the Assyrians under King Nebuchadnezzar. They were followed by the Babylonians in the sixth century B.C., and the Persians who ruled until the fourth century B.C.

Greek and Roman Rule

In the second half of the fourth century B.C., the Greeks under Alexander the Great expanded their empire into the Middle East. One of Alexander's generals, Seleucus, settled in Antioch and started a dynasty that ruled Greater Syria for three centuries. Seleucus expanded Latakia into a major international port. Under his successors, Greek and Syrian cultures blended together and created the Hellenistic culture that is still admired for its developments in law, philosophy, and science.[1]

In 65 B.C., the Roman Army commanded by Pompey conquered Syria and made it a Roman province. Syria became an important economic link in Rome's powerful empire. The trade routes to Asia brought silk from China. Phoenician purple dye was in great demand in Rome. From the Syrian ports, Rome imported grain, fruit, textiles, timber, and resin, among many other products.

In A.D. 324, Emperor Constantine shifted the Roman Empire's capital to Byzantium and named his new capital Constantinople (present-day Istanbul, Turkey). He made Christianity the state religion. Many Arab tribes in Greater Syria were also Christian, including the ruling Ghassanid Arab tribe. In 395, the Roman Empire split in two. The eastern portion of the empire was called the Byzantine Empire.

The Byzantine ruler divided Syria into two provinces. The area north of Homs was called Syria Prima or Major. It had two important cities: the capital, Antioch, in southern Turkey, and Aleppo. The area south of Homs was called the province of Syria Secunda or Phoenicia, and it was divided into two parts. One part was Phoenicia Prima, consisting of much of present-day Lebanon, with Tyre as its capital. The other part was Phoenicia Secunda, with Damascus as its capital city. As a major trade center, Damascus grew into one of the major cities in the Roman Empire.

▷ Arabs in Pre-Islamic Syria

Besides the nomadic tribes, many Arabs in pre-Islamic Syria settled in the towns that were

Queen Zenoba controlled Palmyra during its golden age in the second and third centuries. The Baal Temple (shown here) is part of the ruins making up the ancient city, called the Bride of the Syrian Desert.

expanding rapidly along the trade routes. Many Arabs became part of the Syrian-Byzantine communities. For instance, in parts of the region, Arabs had attained influential positions in town governments.[2]

There were several prominent Arab tribes during the Roman Empire era. The Nabataeans, an Arab tribe with many Christian converts, ruled a small empire from its capital in Petra (in modern-day Jordan). When Pompey defeated the Nabataean king in Damascus in 65 B.C., the Nabataeans became a tribute-paying kingdom. In the second century A.D., the Romans annexed this kingdom as the Roman province of Arabia Petra. At the peak of their power, the Nabataean Arabs controlled much of the sea and land routes to Asia.

Palmyra

Another famous city ruled by Arabs was Palmyra, once known as Tadmor. Although part of the Roman Empire, Palmyra was allowed to govern itself. When war between Rome and Persia heated up in the third century A.D., Palmyra declared independence.

The Palmyran king died in 267. His son was too young to rule, so his widow, Zenobia, took control. Zenobia, who is described as a warrior queen, led Palmyran cavalry and archers into battle against

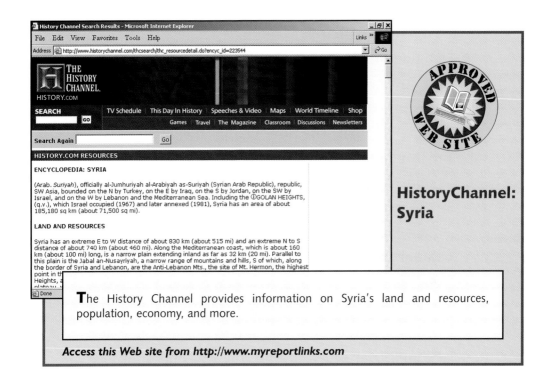

History Channel Search Results - Microsoft Internet Explorer

File   Edit   View   Favorites   Tools   Help   Links »

Address 🔲 http://www.historychannel.com/thcsearch/thc_resourcedetail.do?encyc_id=223544   ▼ ⌀Go

THE
HISTORY
CHANNEL.
HISTORY.COM

SEARCH   TV Schedule   This Day In History   Speeches & Video   Maps   World Timeline   Shop
         GO   Games   Travel   The Magazine   Classroom   Discussions   Newsletters

Search Again [   ]   Go

HISTORY.COM RESOURCES

ENCYCLOPEDIA: SYRIA

(Arab. *Suriyah*), officially al-Jumhuriyah al-Arabiyah as-Suriyah (Syrian Arab Republic), republic,
SW Asia, bounded on the N by Turkey, on the E by Iraq, on the S by Jordan, on the SW by
Israel, and on the W by Lebanon and the Mediterranean Sea. Including the ①GOLAN HEIGHTS,
(q.v.), which Israel occupied (1967) and later annexed (1981), Syria has an area of about
185,180 sq km (about 71,500 sq mi).

LAND AND RESOURCES

Syria has an extreme E to W distance of about 830 km (about 515 mi) and an extreme N to S
distance of about 740 km (about 460 mi). Along the Mediterranean coast, which is about 160
km (about 100 mi) long, is a narrow plain extending inland as far as 32 km (20 mi). Parallel to
this plain is the Jabal an-Nusayriyah, a narrow range of mountains and hills, S of which, along
the border of Syria and Lebanon, are the Anti-Lebanon Mts., the site of Mt. Hermon, the highest
point in th
Heights, a
plateau.

🔲 Done

HistoryChannel: Syria

The History Channel provides information on Syria's land and resources, population, economy, and more.

Access this Web site from http://www.myreportlinks.com

the Roman Empire. By 270, she had conquered much of Greater Syria, including the cities of Alexandria in Egypt and Antioch in Turkey.

In the end, the Roman Army proved too powerful. Zenobia retreated to Palmyra. As Roman armies pursued her, she continued her escape but was finally captured near the Euphrates River. Zenobia's fate is unclear. Some historians say she committed suicide. Others believe Zenobia was taken prisoner and put in chains to appear before the Roman emperor. Some evidence suggests that she married a Roman governor and lived the remainder of her life near the city of Tivoli, north of Rome.[3]

▷ The Rise of Islam

Muhammad's preaching became a unifying force for Arabs. When he died, the elder males of the Muslim community elected Abu Bakr as the first caliph of Islam. The title "caliph" means successor to Muhammad and involves both religious and political leadership.

Abu Bakr sent an army into southern Syria. Their victories launched the expansion of Islam. Under the next caliph, Umar, Damascus and the majority of Byzantine Syria came under the control of the Muslim Arabs. Umar was followed by Uthman of the Umayyad family in Mecca. When Uthman was killed in 656, the Muslims split into different warring factions. Each faction claimed a candidate for caliph. One group in Arabia agreed to appoint Ali, Muhammad's son-in-law and first cousin, as the fourth caliph. Another group in Syria appointed Muawiya, a cousin of Uthman and the governor of Syria.

Ali moved his capital city to Iraq to offset the influence of Muawiya and his family, the Umayyads, who had a strong voice in Damascus. However, Muawiya believed he should be the caliph. Civil war broke out between Ali and Muawiya. Ali eventually conceded to a compromise, allowing Muawiya more power in Syria. However, Ali was assassinated in 661 by a group of dissatisfied Muslims.

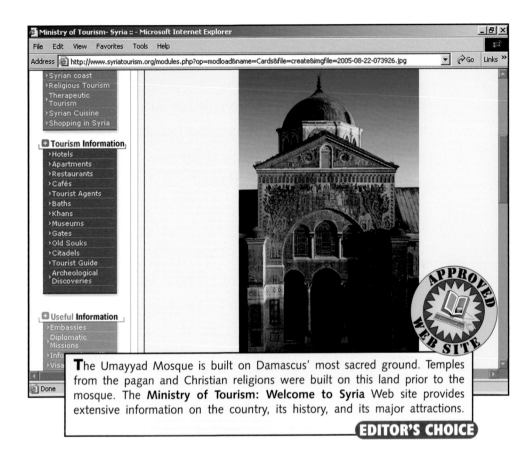

> Syrian coast
> Religious Tourism
> Therapeutic Tourism
> Syrian Cuisine
> Shopping in Syria

⊞ **Tourism Information**
> Hotels
> Apartments
> Restaurants
> Cafés
> Tourist Agents
> Baths
> Khans
> Museums
> Gates
> Old Souks
> Citadels
> Tourist Guide
> Archeological Discoveries

⊞ **Useful Information**
> Embassies
> Diplomatic Missions
> Info
> Visa

The Umayyad Mosque is built on Damascus' most sacred ground. Temples from the pagan and Christian religions were built on this land prior to the mosque. The **Ministry of Tourism: Welcome to Syria** Web site provides extensive information on the country, its history, and its major attractions.

EDITOR'S CHOICE

▷ Umayyad Dynasty

Muawiya declared himself the new caliph from his capital of Damascus. Later on, Ali's two sons, Hasan and Husayn, were killed, causing Ali's supporters to rebel against the Umayyads. They called themselves Shiat Ali, or the party of Ali. Ever since, they have considered themselves separate from the majority of Muslims.

Between 661 and 750, Syria was governed by the Umayyad Arabs. They avoided mixing with the majority of the local people. However, they did not force Islam on people. For instance, Muawiya had a Christian Arab wife.

Before he died, Muawiya made sure his position as caliph was passed on to his son. Shortly thereafter, a civil war erupted among claimants of the caliphate. This war was won by Abd al-Malik, a Umayyad, who declared himself caliph.

An Arab Empire

Within a few decades, the Umayyads had conquered land far beyond Greater Syria. By 750 the Arab Empire included a larger amount of territory than the Roman Empire. From their capital in Damascus, the Umayyads ruled an empire stretching from India to Spain. It included the modern Middle East, Pakistan, and North Africa.

This rapid expansion made it necessary to recruit non-Arabs into the army. Soon these new soldiers began converting to Islam. Conversions to Islam were also popular in the cities where people of many different ethnic and tribal groups mixed. In time, many of the non-Arabs learned to conduct business in Arabic, adopted Arab culture, and converted to Islam.[4]

Legacy of the Umayyad Dynasty

The legacy of the Syrian-based Umayyad dynasty is immense. Caliph Abd al-Malik built the Dome of the Rock in Jerusalem, one of Islam's grandest pieces of architecture. Another famous building, begun in 705 by Abd-al-Malik's son, the caliph al-Walid, was the Umayyad Mosque, also known as the Grande Mosque of Damascus. It was described 280 years later, by the geographer al-Maqdisi as "paved with white marble." Extending to the ceiling were "mosaics of various

△ *Margat overlooks the Mediterranean Sea in Syria. The Knights Hospitalers, a powerful military order of the Crusading Army, used this fortress as its headquarters in Syria.*

colors and in gold, showing figures of trees and towns and beautiful inscriptions."[5]

Many parts of the Umayyad Mosque were destroyed by fires in 1069, 1401, and 1893. But after each fire, Syrians rebuilt and expanded the mosque. Today the mosque's original three minarets and golden dome can be seen from many miles around. The extensive, paved courtyard is surrounded by stone columns that support two stories of rooms. The walls are made from a variety of materials, including colored marble. There are hundreds of rooms in the rectangular building that are used as shrines, religious displays, and rooms for visitors.

▷ Decline of the Damascus-led Empire

Eventually the Umayyads' power declined. Abbas, a descendant of one of Muhammad's uncles, claimed the caliphate in 749. He led a revolt in Persia, defeated the fourteenth Umayyad caliph, and began a new family line of rulers. The second Abbasid caliph founded the city of Baghdad in 762, which served as the capital. Damascus suffered through much of this period. Parts of the city were destroyed by different enemies, and the economy was weak for several hundred years.

Syria became a province in the Abbasid Empire. As long as Syrian governors accepted Abbasid rule, they controlled their own province. But they struggled against constant invasions from the Greeks and Turks in the north and from the Egyptians in the south. A Shi'ite prince in Aleppo established the Hamdani kingdom in northern Syria during the tenth century. Then in 1094, the Seljuk Turks overran the Hamdani kingdom.

Syria During the Crusades

The Seljuks were Turkish nomadic warriors fleeing invasions by the Mongols from central Asia. The Seljuks defeated the Byzantines in 1071. This opened the Byzantine Empire to the Turkish nomads. Many feared the rest of Europe would be overtaken by these Muslims. Several European kings reacted to the fall of the Byzantines by joining the Roman Catholic pope's call for a holy war. Their goal was to conquer Jerusalem and other Christian holy places in the Middle East. They also hoped to create a European kingdom in the Middle East so they could gain huge profits by controlling the region's trade routes and banking.[6]

Between 1095 and 1271, European kings led nine separate military expeditions to the Middle East, known as the Crusades. They occupied a few major coastal cities and Jerusalem in 1099. But mostly the European Crusades failed. Seljuk general Zangi and his son, Nur al-Din, controlled Greater Syria in the mid-twelfth century. Together they led several Muslim offensives against the crusaders. After Nur al-Din's death, his general

▲ Saladin is one of history's most famous Muslim leaders. When he died in Damascus after a brief illness, Saladin was entombed in the Al-Aziziyeh School built by his son, Othman.

in Egypt, a Kurd named Saladin, declared himself the head of a new dynasty, the Ayyubids, with his capital in Cairo.

Saladin recaptured Jerusalem temporarily from the Christian crusaders in 1187. At the same time, he fought against the Seljuks for control of other parts of Greater Syria. Before he died in 1193, Saladin had conquered much of the territory from Persia to the Sudan in Africa. He restored Damascus to its former glory.

Saladin's successors were unable to hold the empire together, however. Soon, Syria was split into small city-states ruled by families in Aleppo, Hama, Homs, and Damascus. The Ayyubids were replaced as the real masters of Egypt by their slave-soldiers, called Mamluks, almost half a century later.

Mamluk Dynasty

In the mid-thirteenth century, the Mongols under Houlagou, the grandson of Genghis Khan, swept into Syria and killed thousands of people. They destroyed much of Damascus. Soon they were driven back by an Egyptian army led by the Mamluks in 1260. The Mamluks' victory marked the end of the Abbasid Empire.

The Mamluks ruled for 250 years. During their reign, prosperity returned to Damascus and Greater Syria. Still, Christian crusader and Mongol invasions kept the Mamluks at war. Considering the Mongols a more serious threat, the Mamluks signed truces with the Christian crusader armies.

By 1291, the Mamluks had crushed the Crusades. In 1399, Tamerlane led a Mongol army that destroyed Damascus. They killed most of the male residents. The remaining citizens finally bribed him with a million pieces of gold to gain their freedom and safety. Tamerlane soon withdrew from Damascus, leaving disorder behind.

▷ Ottoman Empire

In western Turkey, a Muslim Turkish group called the Ottomans began their rise. In 1453 they overran Constantinople, the former capital of the

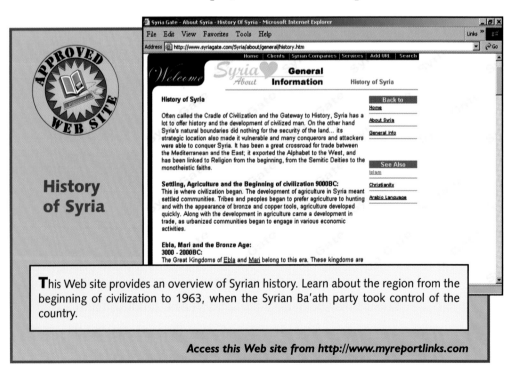

This Web site provides an overview of Syrian history. Learn about the region from the beginning of civilization to 1963, when the Syrian Ba'ath party took control of the country.

Access this Web site from http://www.myreportlinks.com

Byzantine Empire. In the following century, they pushed south into Greater Syria.

In 1516, the Ottoman leader, called the sultan, defeated the Mamluk Army at Aleppo. All of Greater Syria became part of the Ottoman Empire. The sultan divided Greater Syria into three provinces: Aleppo in the north, Tripoli on the coast, and Damascus in the south. Each of the provinces governed smaller units. For example, Damascus was the capital of the area that included Gaza, Nablus, Palmyra, Sido, Beirut, and Jerusalem.

Under the Ottomans, Syria's economy thrived for a couple of centuries. Aleppo and Damascus were revived as crafts and trade expanded. However, by the eighteenth century, the entire region was in decline. Hundreds of villages disappeared, as people migrated into cities away from the desert and raiding Bedouin nomadic tribes. Ottoman troops had to be sent to suppress uprisings by local groups in Lebanon and Egypt.

European Interests in Syria

By the nineteenth century, the Ottoman Empire was crumbling. European powers nicknamed it the "Sick Man of Europe." European nations were expanding their empires into Asia and Africa. However, countries such as Great Britain, France, and Russia believed they would gain profits from

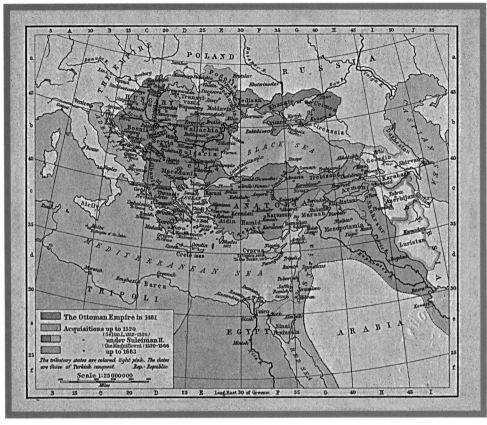

▲ A map of the Ottoman Empire.

Middle Eastern trade only with a unified Ottoman Empire.

France and Great Britain decided to send in forces to stabilize and control the region. In the late eighteenth century, French leader Napoléon Bonaparte temporarily controlled the Egyptian coast. From there he sent an army to conquer Syria. The British countered with troops to support the Syrian governor at the city of Acre in 1799. Napoléon was defeated.

Provincial leaders asserted their independence from the sultan every chance they got. In 1832, Egypt's ruler drove the Ottomans out of Damascus. Fearing that the Egyptian Army would ultimately destroy the Ottoman Empire, Great Britain sent its navy to the Mediterranean. In 1840, the British defeated the Egyptians and returned Syria to the Ottoman Empire.

The French and British also wanted to protect Christian communities in the Ottoman Empire. In 1860, a civil war broke out between the Druze, a Muslim minority, and Christians in the Lebanon Mountains. Disorder spread rapidly to Damascus where Muslims killed thousands of Christians. French troops landed on the Lebanese coast, threatening to intervene. The Ottoman leaders, afraid that the French would take control, agreed to separate much of Lebanon from Syria.

This would be the beginning of European intervention in Syria and other Middle Eastern nations.

Modern History

The Ottoman leaders allied with Germany in World War I. They sent troops to fight the British and French in the Middle East, hoping to drive them out of the region. The British and French, who controlled Algeria, Egypt, and Sudan at that time, were worried that an Ottoman victory in the Middle East might inspire Arab Muslims to rebel

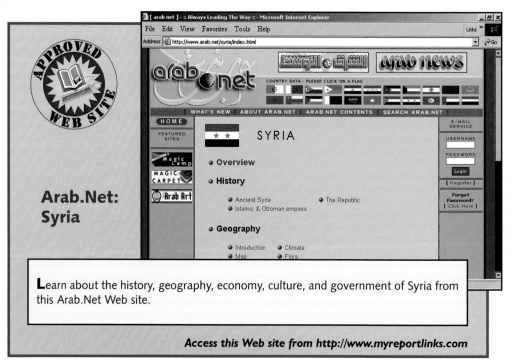

Arab.Net: Syria

Learn about the history, geography, economy, culture, and government of Syria from this Arab.Net Web site.

Access this Web site from http://www.myreportlinks.com

against Europeans. To counter Ottoman influence, British leaders bargained with Sharif Hussein, the leader of Mecca, for his support.

Hussein agreed to fight the Ottoman Turks, and in return, the British promised him an independent Arab nation after the war. In June 1916, Hussein's army, commanded by his son, Prince Faisal, led an Arab revolt against the Ottomans. With help from British military advisors such as T. E. Lawrence (also known as Lawrence of Arabia), Prince Faisal led his victorious troops into Damascus in October 1918.

Post-World War I events, however, disappointed Arab leaders. The Versailles Peace Conference in 1919 failed to grant independence to Syria. A dissatisfied Prince Faisal returned from the conference as the king of Syria under the short-lived British control of the area, which began in 1918.

▷ Sykes-Picot Agreement

Great Britain and France had already made secret plans for dividing up the Middle East between them in the 1916 Sykes-Picot Agreement. The French would control Syria and Lebanon, and the British would control Iraq, Jordan, and Palestine. They also agreed to support an independent Arab state or confederation.

The Sykes-Picot Agreement would conflict with the mandate system created by the League of Nations after World War I. The League of Nations gave countries, such as Great Britain and France, mandates over territories to guide toward independence. Territories classified as Class A mandates, such as Lebanon, Iraq, Jordan, Palestine, and Syria, were considered ready for independence with administrative advice and assistance.

▶ French Mandate

In March 1920, King Faisal met with Syrian and Iraqi leaders. They declared unconditional independence for both nations. They also claimed that territories still controlled by the British and the French, especially Palestine, were within Syria's boundaries.[1] Therefore they considered the territories to be a part of Syria.

The French sent in troops to take control of Faisal's forces. Although Arab soldiers resisted, Damascus fell quickly in July 1920. Faisal fled to England, and Syria was governed as a French protectorate. As a concession to Arab nationalism, Great Britain named Faisal king of the territory of Iraq in 1921.

The French divided up Greater Syria into two territories: Lebanon and Syria. Lebanon consisted of the Mount Lebanon region in the south and the coastal area northward past Tripoli. Syria was divided into five states: Alexandretta (part of present-day Turkey), Aleppo, Latakia, Damascus, and Jabal Druze.

▶ Syrian Nationalism

Syrian nationalists accused France of violating the League of Nations Mandate. In this agreement, France had given its word to grant independence to Syria. When the British allowed Iraqis to elect their own national assembly in 1924, Syrians demanded the same. The French permitted Syrian leaders to organize a political party called the People's party (PP). Reluctantly, the French combined the Aleppo and Damascus provinces into one large Arab state, hoping Syrians would think this was a step toward independence.

Syrians wanted more, however. Anti-French demonstrations continued. In 1925, Sultan Pasha al-Atrash led a successful Druze uprising in the southwest, and fighting spread to Damascus. The French bombed parts of the city, killing nearly five thousand Syrians. An uneasy truce followed.

In 1930, France allowed Syrian leaders to form the National Bloc alliance and the Independence party. The alliance

The Lure of Aleppo

Access this Web site from http://www.myreportlinks.com

Aleppo is the second largest city in Syria and one of the oldest cities in the world. Read about Aleppo's long history at this Web site.

wrote a constitution that led to the election of a Syrian parliament and president. Syrian officials then asked that Lebanon and Syria be reunited. The French refused, and more disorders broke out. Unhappy with the lack of progress toward self-rule, Syrian president Hashim al-Atassi resigned in 1939. That same year, the French suspended the constitution.

▷ Drive to Independence

When World War II broke out, France had little time to look after its colonies. Therefore, the French authorities turned over more governing responsibilities

◁ *In 1943, General Charles de Gaulle, co-president of the transitional French government, announced that Syria would be given its independence. As a way of prolonging French control over the area, he also said that Syrian independence would not happen until a new French government put an end to the League of Nations Mandate.*

to native officials. In 1943, Syrians elected a new parliament and president. French leader Charles de Gaulle then announced that Syria would be given its independence soon.

By 1944, the Syrians were running most of the government. The United States and the Union of Soviet Socialist Republics (USSR) recognized Syria as an independent nation, and Great Britain did so in 1945. As a sovereign nation, Syria declared war on Germany, Italy, and Japan. Syria also became a charter member of the United Nations.

Even after most nations recognized Syrian independence, French forces stayed. The French government wanted to hold on to its military and economic control over the Middle East as long as possible. Demonstrations against the French broke out in Damascus and Aleppo. The French retaliated by bombing Damascus and fighting Syrians in other cities.

▷ The End of Colonialism

Fearing that disorder in Syria would endanger British plans for a peaceful settlement in its territories of Iraq and Palestine, British prime minister Winston Churchill stepped in and threatened to send British troops against the French. As a result, General de Gaulle declared a cease-fire, and by April 17, 1946, all French troops were gone.

Winston Churchill, Great Britain's prime minister, stepped in before Charles de Gaulle incited an all out war in Syria.

The Syrians were bitter about their treatment by the French during the colonial period. Many of Syria's leaders were determined to unite all the Arab people under a single Arab state.[2] Colonialism gave rise to the modern-day concept of Arab unity. The Ba'ath (Arab Socialist Resurrection) party that rules Syria today took its cues from the Arab struggle against colonialism.

Palestine and Israel: Roots of the Conflict

Arab nationalism was only one factor that has made the Middle East a center of conflict since World War II. The Arabs intensely resisted a British plan to give Jewish immigrants their own state in Palestine.

In the mid-nineteenth century, there were only about twelve thousand Jews living in Palestine. By 1914, there were nearly eighty-five thousand, many fleeing persecution in Russia and Eastern

Europe. These immigrants believed in the Zionist ideology that declared Palestine a home for all Jews. In 1917, the British government issued the Balfour Declaration promising land in Palestine to Jews around the world for their own independent nation. Riots erupted between the Arab and Jewish immigrant communities throughout the 1930s as Arabs protested the British plan as well as the rising number of Jewish immigrants to Palestine.

The 1948–49 War

In 1945, the League of Arab States (The Arab League) was created by Egypt, Iraq, Lebanon, Saudi Arabia, Syria, Transjordan (present-day Jordan), and Yemen. The Palestinian Arabs were also given full membership, although they had no independent nation-state. The organization's goal was to unify Arab nations economically and politically and to halt Zionist Jewish expansion in Palestine. In 1947, the United Nations took over Palestine and ordered that the country be divided into Jewish and Arab states. The UN wanted to place Jerusalem under its control. Palestinian Arabs rioted against the plan. In May 1948, Arab armies, totaling about twenty-five thousand soldiers, from Egypt, Transjordan, Syria, Lebanon, and Iraq invaded Palestine after the declaration of the establishment of the Jewish state of Israel.

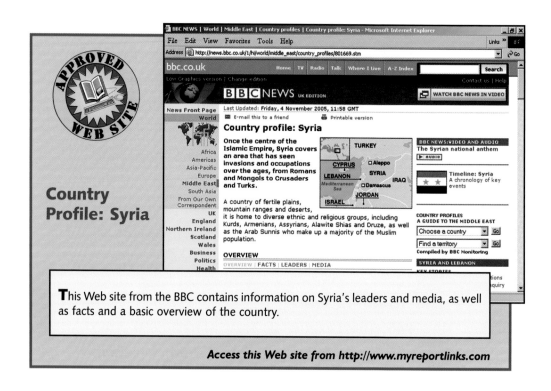

Country
Profile: Syria

This Web site from the BBC contains information on Syria's leaders and media, as well as facts and a basic overview of the country.

Access this Web site from http://www.myreportlinks.com

The Arab nations were quickly defeated by the larger Israeli Army. The Jewish nation of Israel was recognized by most countries in the world. After this first Arab-Israeli War, Israel occupied much more territory than assigned by the original UN plan.

Political Parties

In 1948, Syrian leaders were mainly landowners, industrialists, and merchants who had inherited their money and prominent positions. They had no experience running an independent country.

Two major political parties ran Syria. The National party (NP), with its support based in

Damascus, was in control of the government. The NP tended to emphasize industrial growth and looked to Palestine and Lebanon as its close partners. In contrast, the People's party drew political support from landlords in Aleppo. The PP stressed agricultural development and favored unity with Iraq and Jordan.

Even though it had been founded in 1940 by two philosophy professors at Damascus University, Michael Aflaq and Salah al-Din al-Bitar, the Ba'ath party was just emerging as a political force. Most of the Ba'ath party's membership came from the new middle class of professionals, such as teachers and public employees. Originally the Ba'ath party was based on Arab nationalism. However, in 1962, it was challenged by the Socialist party, causing the Ba'ath party to alter its position. From then on, the party called for a moderate form of socialism to modernize the Arab world.

▷ The First Military Coup

The military blamed Syria's civilian leadership for the Arabs' loss of the 1948–49 Arab-Israeli War. In addition, high inflation and widespread government corruption was eroding public support for the leaders.

In 1949, General Husni az-Zaim took over Syria's government in the first of many military coups d'état. The military favored the Ba'ath party

Country at a Glance: Lebanon

Access this Web site from http://www.myreportlinks.com

Get information on Lebanon's economy, health technology, and more from the United Nations. Links to updated news sources are also included.

because of its strong pan-Arab position and its neutral attitude toward religion. By the 1950s, the Ba'ath party had become one of the most powerful political parties in Syria, along with the Syrian Communist party and the Muslim Brotherhood.

United Arab Republic

Ba'ath leaders believed that joining in an Arab federation with anti-Communist Egypt would damage Communist support. In February 1958, Syria and Egypt formed the United Arab Republic (UAR). Egypt insisted that the two nations be under a single government. Gamal Abdul Nasser of Egypt took over the presidency of the UAR, and Egyptians replaced many Syrian administrators.

Nasser treated Syria as a province of Egypt. Dissatisfied with the arrangement, a group of military officers formed a secret organization later called the Military Committee, within the Ba'ath party. Although the organization's members represented many sections of Syria, the majority was made up of non-Sunni Muslims. They were members of minority groups. The Alawis dominated the Military Committee, and Hafiz al-Assad was one of the more active Alawi officers.

The officers wanted to restore Syrian independence. In September 1961, the military staged another coup and took over the government in Damascus. They immediately pulled Syria out of the UAR. A long period of chaos followed in Syria. The army was divided into pro-Nasser and pro-Syria groups. Throughout the spring of 1963, these and other groups fought in the streets of Damascus. In July, the army under the command of Major General Amin al-Hafiz, a Sunni, took control of the government.

The Rise of Hafiz al-Assad

Much of the new government consisted of Ba'ath party members. An older, more traditional group of Ba'ath members, led by Michael Aflaq and Amin al-Hafiz, favored a moderate pace of socialism. The more radical group, including Salah Jadid and Hafiz al-Assad, pushed for a quicker pace to socialism. Amin al-Hafiz was unable to maintain public order, and over the next two years the Syrian government changed hands frequently.

In February 1966, Amin al-Hafiz was planning to dismiss about thirty minority officers from the government. Jadid, head of the Ba'ath party and a Druze, found out and staged a coup. Jadid became

the most powerful man in Syria, and he named
Assad head of the air force and minister of defense.

Six-Day War and its Aftermath

In June 1967, Israel invaded its Arab neighbors
and won a quick victory in the Six-Day War. As a
result, Syria lost possession of the Golan Heights.
Afterwards, Jadid and Assad clashed over policy.

An older Hafiz al-Assad arrives in Paris in 1998—two years before his death.
President al-Assad controlled Syria as a dictator for thirty years, from 1970 to 2000.

Their most serious disagreement concerned support for Palestinian refugee groups in Jordan that made up the Palestinian Liberation Organization (PLO). The PLO had been carrying out guerrilla attacks on Israel. When Jordan's King Hussein expelled the PLO from his country in 1970, refugees set up camps in Lebanon.

In the fighting between the PLO and the Jordanians, Syria's leaders were divided on their support. In September 1970, Jadid sent in two hundred tanks to back the PLO. However, Assad, head of the Syrian Air Force, refused to send planes to protect the tanks. Defenseless against Jordanian planes, Syrian tanks retreated.

Jadid's failure in the Jordanian war led to another coup. This time, Hafiz al-Assad took over the government in a bloodless coup on November 13, 1970. Assad became prime minister and minister of defense, making him the most powerful person in Syria.

The Hafiz al-Assad Regime

Hafiz al-Assad changed the course of Syrian politics. Using his military base and broad powers, Assad kept his government together for thirty years. After reorganizing the Ba'ath party, Assad arranged for a referendum on the new government. His nomination for president of the country was approved by the people in March 1971.

Assad held dictatorial powers. In 1973, he pushed through a constitution that established the present system of governing Syria. Many people opposed his methods, but they had no power to act.

Peaceful opposition from intellectuals and former government officials surfaced in 1980. They called themselves the National Democratic Gathering. Among this group's demands were basic democratic rights that were enjoyed in Western countries—freedom of the press, freedom to organize political parties, the end of the state

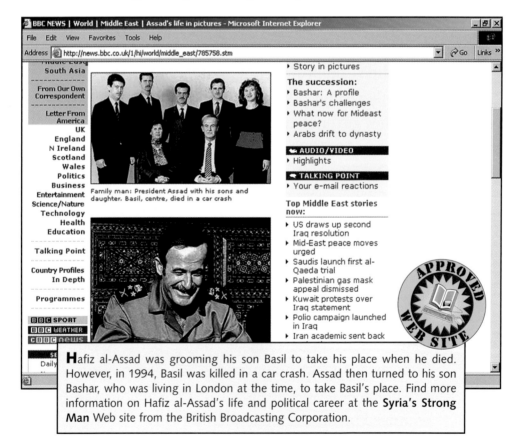

Hafiz al-Assad was grooming his son Basil to take his place when he died. However, in 1994, Basil was killed in a car crash. Assad then turned to his son Bashar, who was living in London at the time, to take Basil's place. Find more information on Hafiz al-Assad's life and political career at the **Syria's Strong Man** Web site from the British Broadcasting Corporation.

of emergency, and free elections.[3] However, the Assad regime also faced militant opposition such as the Muslim Brotherhood.

Palestinian Refugees

During his regime, Assad directed much of his attention to the Palestinian refugee problem. He considered Israel's occupation of the Palestinians' homeland as the central problem in the Middle East. He wanted Syria to lead the Arabs in a war to drive the Jews out of Israel.

However, Assad's armies were no match for the Israeli military. In 1973, Egypt, Jordan, and Syria tried to regain territory lost in the 1967 war with no success. Israel continued occupying the Golan Heights, Sinai, and the Gaza Strip. Since that time, approximately thirteen hundred UN peacekeeping forces have patrolled the border between Syria and the Golan Heights.

A million Palestinian refugees were living in southern Lebanon. Instead of looking to Assad for leadership, they generally followed Yasir Arafat and the PLO. However, Assad considered himself the true spokesman of the Palestinian refugees. They were, he believed, part of the greater Arab nation that should include Palestine, Lebanon, Jordan, and Syria.

When Lebanon's government was threatened by the PLO in 1976, Assad accepted Lebanon's call for military assistance. More than thirty thousand Syrian troops were stationed in Lebanon as representatives of the United Nation's peacekeeping efforts. In 1989, Syria signed the Taif Agreement with Lebanon. According to the treaty, Syria was supposed to withdraw its troops. However, Syria refused to withdraw until Israel pulled its troops out of the Golan Heights. When Assad died in June 2000, Syrian troops were still in Lebanon.

▷ Bashar al-Assad

Hafiz al-Assad's son, Bashar, was only thirty-four years old at the time of his father's death. Bashar immediately assumed the presidency. Then in a

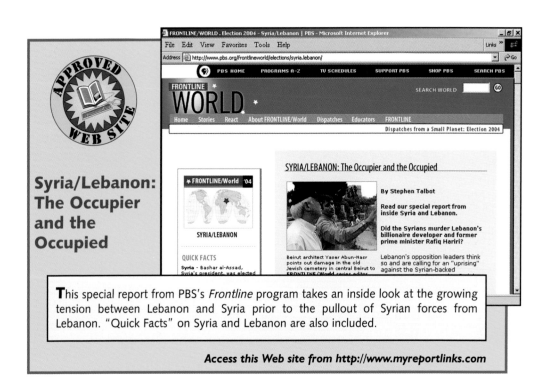

Syria/Lebanon: The Occupier and the Occupied

This special report from PBS's *Frontline* program takes an inside look at the growing tension between Lebanon and Syria prior to the pullout of Syrian forces from Lebanon. "Quick Facts" on Syria and Lebanon are also included.

Access this Web site from http://www.myreportlinks.com

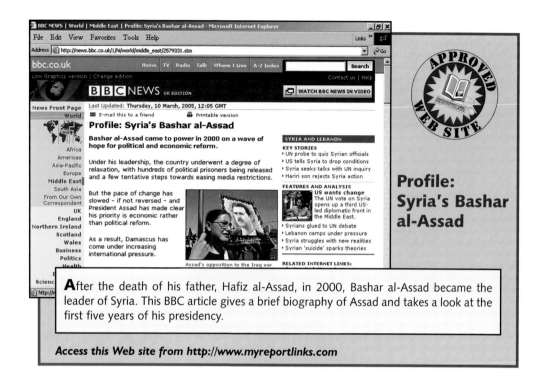

After the death of his father, Hafiz al-Assad, in 2000, Bashar al-Assad became the leader of Syria. This BBC article gives a brief biography of Assad and takes a look at the first five years of his presidency.

Access this Web site from http://www.myreportlinks.com

national referendum, the people voted to give Bashar the presidency for a seven-year term.

During his early years as president, Bashar has tried to de-emphasize his conflicts with neighboring countries. Instead, he has sought to build up Syria's weak economy by diversifying its industries.

Economy

Syria is a poor nation by any standard. The median monthly income per person is less than one hundred dollars.[1] To support a typical Syrian family of five to six members, the household spends, on average, more than two hundred dollars a month.[2] Unemployment ranges between 15 to 25 percent annually, compared to an average of about 5 percent in the United States. It is complicated by the large number of young people who enter the job market every year. To provide jobs for these people and develop the nation, Syria's economy needs to grow about 7 percent annually. Instead, the economy has averaged less than 3 percent annual growth for several years.

Most of the country's economic growth is financed by the oil industry. While Syria has some oil reserves, its oil supply has been rapidly declining since 1996. This caused oil production and exports to decline. Meanwhile, Syria charges transit fees for allowing oil pipelines from other countries to cross Syrian land.

Syrian officials are aware that their socialist policies protect money-losing industries. The government owns and controls the major industries, employs the most workers, and owns and regulates the entire financial section of the economy. Even though private businesses and farms operate in Syria, they are also under government supervision.[3]

Overview of the Economy

For the first decade of independence, Syria's economy grew steadily. However, the people who benefited most were wealthy urban merchants who could invest in land. The vast majority of

▲ *A Syrian merchant displays his wares in the marketplace.*

people were peasants. In the first step of their socialist program, the Ba'ath party passed laws in the 1960s that freed up some land for poor farmers. Then most industries were nationalized. This means that they were placed under government ownership and control.

The main stimulant for the economy in the 1970s came from oil. Income from oil exports helped finance new roads, dams, irrigation projects, and industrial plants. In the 1970s, the Syrian economy grew nearly 10 percent a year. However, the world market prices for oil dropped continuously in the 1980s. As a result, Syria began suffering huge budget deficits. The government was unable to pay its debts to other nations. The economy remained weak until the 1990s when oil prices began rising again.

▶ Government Control

Between 1961 and 1990, Syria's government services expanded faster than any other economic sector. The Assad government built and operated hundreds of new schools, hospitals, and social services. During this period, the government also built and operated dams and electrical power plants in many parts of the country. This government control, as well as corruption, has brought hardship to Syria, especially during the 1980s.

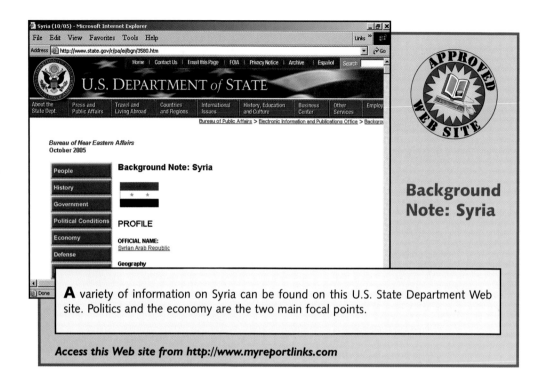

A variety of information on Syria can be found on this U.S. State Department Web site. Politics and the economy are the two main focal points.

Access this Web site from http://www.myreportlinks.com

▷ Farm Cooperatives

In 1963, seven out of ten Syrian farms were larger than twenty acres. The Ba'ath party took control of the government and immediately passed a land reform law. Small plots of land were offered to farmers, and by 1975, the vast majority of Syrian farms were less than 20 acres.[4] The government took over most of the land and offered to sell plots to farmers at low interest rates if they joined state-sponsored cooperatives. By 1984, there were more than 4,000 agricultural cooperatives with more than 440,000 members.

Farm cooperatives are organizations that are formed by people so they can share work and machines. Farmers who join agree to pay the organization for twenty years to gain ownership of the land. Cooperative officials collect the crops at a central location. Then they send the crops to government-owned plants that process the crops. Each cooperative is like a small community. The central office supplies farm machinery, financial credit, and other services to the farmers. In addition, cooperatives build schools, health clinics, and cultural centers.

Even with favorable laws, however, most Syrian farmers preferred not to join cooperatives. They preferred to own or rent small plots and remain independent. The majority rented their land from landlords or from the government. In 2004, 95 percent of Syrian farms were still privately owned.[5]

Agriculture

Agricultural activities produce more than 30 percent of Syria's wealth. This is higher than any other economic sector. A large portion of Syria's exports, manufacturing plants, trade and commerce, many service industries, and a large number of workers are connected to agriculture, according to economist Alexander Sarris.[6]

The major problem for Syrian farmers is finding an adequate water supply. Farming is a difficult life in a country that has so little rainfall.

Only about one fifth of the farms receive irrigation, so the remaining farms must rely on seasonal rains and underground water supplies. As more manufacturing plants and service industries are built in urban areas, many people leave their farms to live in cities. Between 1970 and 1985, the labor force employed in agriculture dropped from 50 percent to 30 percent.

Herding and fishing make up a small portion of Syria's economy. The nomadic Bedouin graze sheep and goats in the semiarid areas. (Making up less than 7 percent of the nation's population, Bedouins are among the poorest people in the country.)

△ People walk through Aleppo's vaulted suq, or market. Many of Aleppo's suqs have a fountain in the center and date as far back as the fifteenth century.

Most farmers raise animals to supplement their diets and income. The government offers them aid if they raise sheep, goats, and cattle. However, Syria still has to import meat and dairy products.

Artisans and Handicrafters

Syria has a large number of artisans and handicrafters. They spend much of their time in market stalls selling embroidered clothes, jewelry, carpets, and pottery, as well as everyday items, such as soap and shoes. Today their products have to compete with imported goods made with cheaper materials and products mass-produced in local factories.

All the major cities, especially Aleppo and Damascus, have areas where shops and stalls of artisans can be found. Bazaars, or markets, are often specialized. In Damascus, silk clothing is made and sold at the Harir Suq (market), leather goods at the Kuya Suq, and jewelry at the es-Sagha Suq. The most famous market of Damascus is the Suq al-Hamadiyah. It consists of several miles of back alleys where artisans work at crafts. Sounds of hammering come from rooms where brass and copper are being pounded into utensils. The famous Damascus carpets are woven in back rooms of shops. Along the narrow streets, men and women try to lure customers into their shops. Inside, they sell elaborate jewelry of ivory, inlaid with precious stones.

▷ Manufacturing

Before World War II, very little industry existed in Syria except for traditional handicrafters and artisans. After the war, wealthy Syrians started up small industries that processed locally grown crops and made consumer goods. In the 1950s, Syrian industries grew rapidly. However, after taking power in 1963, the Ba'ath party began nationalizing most of the large manufacturing plants. By 1970, 108 enterprises were placed under the control of the Ministry of Industry. They were divided into four major sections: food, textiles, chemicals, and engineering (appliances and electronics). In the 1980s and 1990s, Hafiz al-Assad encouraged

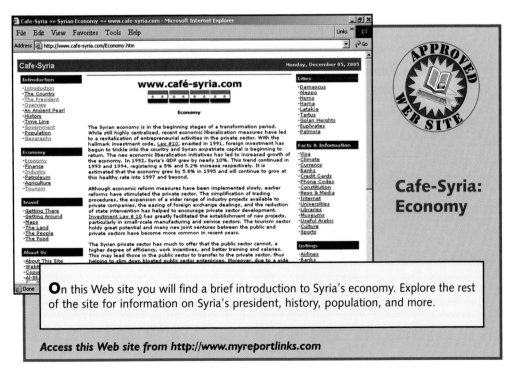

On this Web site you will find a brief introduction to Syria's economy. Explore the rest of the site for information on Syria's president, history, population, and more.

Access this Web site from http://www.myreportlinks.com

more private investments. However, in 2002, the government still owned more than one hundred companies.

Under the influence of government socialist policies, Syrian industrial growth over time has been mixed. Today, manufacturing makes up about 29 percent of the economic activity of the country. One of the obstacles to industrial growth is the central government's ownership of many

of the large industries. Government-owned plants that do not make a profit receive government money to make up their losses. Because of these extra payments, the government has little money left over to invest in building roads, expanding irrigation, modernizing agriculture, and opening new industries.

◁ Although the textile industry is one of Syria's strongest economic sectors, the Syrian government reported in 2004 that the state-run industry has lost about $32 million in recent years.

Oil and Gas

The oil and gas industry is government owned and operated. Well over half of the nation's income from exports comes from oil. However, annual production has declined since 1996 because the amount of known oil in the country is decreasing. Experts predict that Syria may have to begin importing oil by 2010. Income from the oil industry has also been lost from the shutdown of oil pipelines from Iraq after the United States invasion of that country.

Public Companies

With more than 1.3 million employees, Syria's government is the country's single largest employer. Besides the nationalized industries and defense, people work in services such as banking, communications, hospitality, insurance, and retail. President Bashar al-Assad is trying to encourage public industries to make a profit and not depend on the government for financial help. However he is not eliminating very many public companies, and these companies are still inefficient and unprofitable.

Ba'ath Party Reform

President Assad and Ba'ath party leaders believe that controlled, slow reform will prevent social chaos. They point to the instability of Syrian

Syrian president Bashar al-Assad conducts a meeting at the presidential palace in Damascus. Get the latest news from Syria and the surrounding countries of the Middle East from the **Syrian Arab News Agency** Web site.

politics after independence. Between 1949 and 1970, there were more than a dozen successful coups and several more attempts at overthrowing the government. Ba'ath leaders maintain that Syria needed to end the constant fighting and instability in order to begin building a strong, unified nation. And Assad wants to be in complete control over any reform.[7]

When Bashar al-Assad took power in 2000, he found widespread corruption in the government. In addition, the economy was barely growing. It needed basic reform. In response, Assad declared that his priorities were modernizing the economy and cleaning up corruption.

Many Ba'ath officials who have made fortunes from their connections to government over the decades resisted President Assad's moves. As a result, some Western experts question his ability to lead the party.

▷ Syria's Economic Future

Trying to keep a stable society in Syria has proven difficult. In the past, Syria blamed all of its problems on Israel, whether real or imagined. However, with the Palestinian problem closer to solution, Syria can spend more time concentrating on its own internal problems.

In June 2005, the Ba'ath party held its first national assembly since 2000. Assad emphasized economic reforms in his address to the party. He expressed a desire to allow more freedoms, but with caution. Ba'ath party spokeswoman Buthaina Shaaban explained the party's intent: "[W]ith the privatisation we want to make, we also want to ensure that people have good health and education. So it is with social care that we want to approach the economy."[8]

Report Links

The Internet sites described below can be accessed at http://www.myreportlinks.com

▶**Country at a Glance: Syrian Arab Republic**
Editor's Choice Information on Syria from the United Nations.

▶**Ministry of Tourism: Welcome to Syria**
Editor's Choice Read about what you can see and do in Syria.

▶**Perry-Castañeda Library Map Collection: Syria Maps**
Editor's Choice View present-day and historical maps of Syria.

▶**Syria Daily**
Editor's Choice Read the daily news from Syria and the Middle East.

▶**Damascus Online: Everything Syrian**
Editor's Choice Learn about Syrian history on this Web site.

▶**Background on Syria and the Rafiq Hariri Investigation**
Editor's Choice Learn about Syria and the assassination of Rafik Hariri.

▶**Alawis**
On this Web site you will find out more about the Alawis.

▶**Arab.Net: Syria**
This Web site provides general information on Syria.

▶**Background Note: Syria**
Travelers to Syria should check out this site from the U.S. State Department.

▶**BBC News: Middle East**
Read the latest news from Syria and the Middle East.

▶**Cafe-Syria: Economy**
You will find information on Syria's economy on this Web site.

▶**CNN: World/Middle East**
Get the latest news from the Middle East.

▶**Country at a Glance: Lebanon**
Learn about Syria's neighbor, Lebanon.

▶**Country Profile: Syria**
Examine a profile of Syria.

▶**FIFA World Cup: Germany 2006: Syria**
Learn about Syria and its national soccer team.

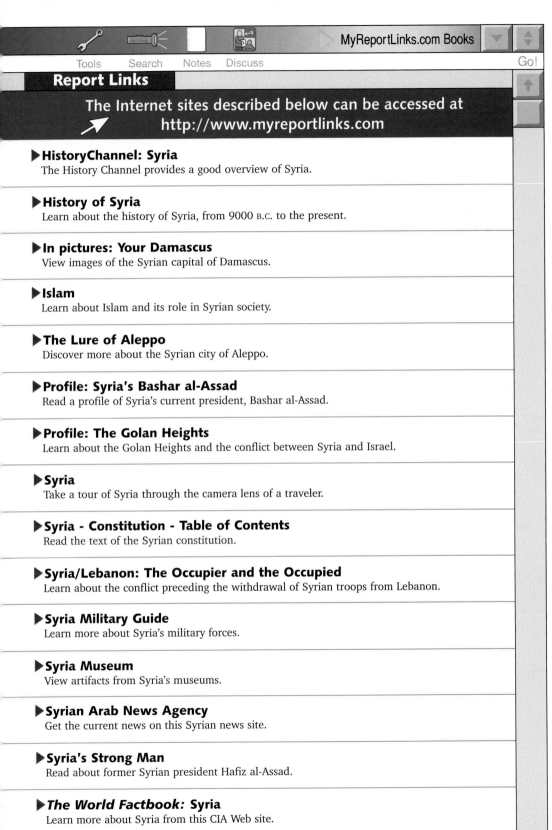

Report Links

The Internet sites described below can be accessed at http://www.myreportlinks.com

▶**HistoryChannel: Syria**
The History Channel provides a good overview of Syria.

▶**History of Syria**
Learn about the history of Syria, from 9000 B.C. to the present.

▶**In pictures: Your Damascus**
View images of the Syrian capital of Damascus.

▶**Islam**
Learn about Islam and its role in Syrian society.

▶**The Lure of Aleppo**
Discover more about the Syrian city of Aleppo.

▶**Profile: Syria's Bashar al-Assad**
Read a profile of Syria's current president, Bashar al-Assad.

▶**Profile: The Golan Heights**
Learn about the Golan Heights and the conflict between Syria and Israel.

▶**Syria**
Take a tour of Syria through the camera lens of a traveler.

▶**Syria - Constitution - Table of Contents**
Read the text of the Syrian constitution.

▶**Syria/Lebanon: The Occupier and the Occupied**
Learn about the conflict preceding the withdrawal of Syrian troops from Lebanon.

▶**Syria Military Guide**
Learn more about Syria's military forces.

▶**Syria Museum**
View artifacts from Syria's museums.

▶**Syrian Arab News Agency**
Get the current news on this Syrian news site.

▶**Syria's Strong Man**
Read about former Syrian president Hafiz al-Assad.

▶***The World Factbook:* Syria**
Learn more about Syria from this CIA Web site.

Alawi—The largest minority group in Syria, originally considered a breakaway group of the Shi'ites. The Alawis have been the most powerful group in Syrian politics since the 1960s.

almsgiving—The third pillar of Islam, it is called zakat in Arabic. Those who can afford it pay 2.5 percent of their wealth annually to charity.

Ba'ath party—A political party formed in 1940. It became the ruling party in Syria in the 1960s. Although all ethnic and religious groups are represented in its membership, minority groups dominate the party, especially the Alawis.

Bedouin—Also Beduin. Nomadic herders, usually referring to Arab ethnic tribes.

caliph—The title of the Sunni religious leader and the civil ruler of the Ottoman Empire until the 1920s.

chador—This is a long cloth worn by conservative Muslim women that wraps around the hair and body.

creed—Called shahada in Arabic, this is the statement that there is only one God, Allah, and Muhammad is his prophet. One of the Five Pillars of Islam.

coup d'état—The sudden and often violent overthrow of a government by a small group.

Druze—The third largest religious group in Syria. Its members live mostly in southern Syria. Their beliefs are a mixture of Islam, Christianity, and other religions, although they are usually classified as a subgroup of the Shi'ites.

Greater Syria—This term is used by many experts to describe the Near East before the twentieth century. It includes the general area that consists of modern-day Syria, Lebanon, Jordan, and Israel.

guerrillas—Soldiers who wage a "hidden" war, launching surprise attacks and then retreating.

hajj—The pilgrimage Muslims must make to Mecca, Saudi Arabia, once a lifetime if they are financially and physically able. One of the five pillars of Islam.

imam—A man considered well educated in Islam. He often has a leadership position at a mosque where he leads group prayer and acts as a religious counselor.

hijab—A scarf that many Muslim women wear around the head to cover their hair.

mandate—An order by the League of Nations to a member nation to oversee the creation of a responsible government in a conquered territory.

monotheism—The belief in one supreme god.

polytheism—The belief in more than one god.

prayer—In Arabic, salah. One of the Five Pillars of Islam. Muslims pray five times a day: at dawn, noon, afternoon, sunset, and after sunset.

referendum—A form of voting by the people that usually allows them to approve or reject a government law or the nomination of an official.

sharia—The system of Islamic laws and teachings that Muslims follow.

Shi'ite—Also Shi'a. The term used to identify the minority group of Muslims who believe that only family descendants of Muhammad should become leaders of the Muslim world. They also believe this leader is the only genuine imam.

socialism—A political theory supporting government ownership of industry.

steppe—The semiarid areas of treeless plains located in Europe and Asia.

Sunni—This is the major group of Muslims. In general they believed that the leader of the Islamic world—the caliph—should be elected, rather than inherit his position. They also follow the Sunnah, which consists of traditions about Muhammad's life.

Syria Facts

1. *exxun.com,* 2005, <http://www.exxun.com/Syria/a_fg.html]> (October 13, 2005).

Chapter 1. Current Events in Syrian News

1. Quoted in Steven R. Weisman, "U.S. Seems Sure of the Hand of Syria, Hinting at Penalties," *The New York Times,* February 15, 2005, Late Edition—Final, Section A, p. 6.

2. Jim Lobe, "Deadliest Year in Palestinian Territories Since 1967 War," *Common Dreams News Center,* January 1, 2002, <http://www.commondreams.org/cgi-bin/print.cgi?file=/headlines02/0101-01.htm> (October 14, 2005).

3. U.S. Department of State, "Background Note: Syria," *Bureau of Near Eastern Affairs,* August 2004, <http://www.state.gov/r/pa/ei/bgn/3580.htm> (November 23, 2005).

4. George W. Bush, "STATE OF THE UNION; 'We Must Pass Reforms That Solve the Financial Problems of Social Security,'" *The New York Times,* February 3, 2005, Late Edition - Final, Section A, p. 22.

5. Center for Nonproliferation Studies, Monterey, California, "Weapons of Mass Destruction in the Middle East," *Monterey Institute of International Studies,* 1998, <http://cns.miis.edu/research/wmdme/syria.htm#2> (February 15, 2005).

Chapter 2. Land and Climate

1. Joshua M. Landis, "Travel to the Syrian Coast," *SyriaComment.com,* April 2, 2005, <http://faculty-staff.ou.edu/L/Joshua.M.Landis-1/syriablog/2005/04/travel-to-syrian-coast.htm> (October 14, 2005).

2. Cass Gilbert, "September 21st: Meeting up with Nick, Aleppo, Syria," Journal, September 21, 2000, <http://www.cyclesydneylondon.com/diary/000921 .html> (June 13, 2005).

3. Lynn Simarski, "The Lure of Aleppo," *Armaco World Magazine,* vol. 38, no. 4, July–August 1987, p. 39.

4. Philip K. Hitti, "The Imperial Capital," *Aramco World Magazine,* vol. 24, no.5, September/October 1973, p. 18, <http://www.saudiaramcoworld.com/issue/197305/the.imperial.capital.htm> (May 16, 2005).

5. "The Early Syria Tour, October 2001," *Palestine Exploration Fund,* December 27, 2004, <http://www.pef.org.uk/EarlySyriaPages/Damascus.htm> (March 13, 2005).

6. Norman N. Lewis, *Nomads and Settlers in Syria and Jordan 1800–1980* (Cambridge: Cambridge University Press, 1987), p. 1.

Chapter 3. Religion

1. Bernard Lewis, *The Arabs in History* (New York: Harper & Row, 1966), p. 47.

2. Erica Fraser, "The Caliphate and the First Islamic Dynasty: Umayyad Politics and Administration," *The Islamic World to 1600,* Tutorial, The Applied History Research Group, University of Calgary, December 6, 2001, <http://www.ucalgary.ca/applied_history/tutor/islam/caliphate/> (June 19, 2005).

3. Mohammed Marmaduke Pickthall, trans., Qur'an, chapter 3, verses 31 and 32, *The Meaning of The Glorious Koran* (New York: New American Library, n.d.), p. 65.

4. John L. Esposito, *Islam: The Straight Path* (New York: Oxford University Press, 1988), p. 90.

5. Joshua M. Landis, "Islamic Education in Syria: Undoing Secularism," "Constructs of Inclusion and Exclusion: Religion and Identity Formation in Middle Eastern School Curricula," *Watson Institute for International Studies, Brown University,* November 2003, <http:// faculty-staff.ou.edu/L/Joshua.M.Landis-1/Islamic%20Education%20in%20Syria.htm#_edn1> (June 8, 2005).

6. Michael Jacobson, "An Islamist Syria Is Not Very Probable," *Washington Institute for Near East Policy,* April 29, 2005, <http://www.washingtoninstitute.org/templateC06.php?CID=823> (June 1, 2005).

Chapter 4. Syrian Culture

1. Robert Scott Mason, "Chapter 2—The Society and Its Environment: Structure of Society," *Syria: A Country Study,* Thomas Collelo, ed. (Washington: GPO for the Library of Congress, 1988), p. 71.

2. International Center for Agricultural Research in the Dry Areas (ICARDA), "Household Livelihood Strategies in Rural Syria: How do Women Contribute?" Annual Report 2000, <http://www.icarda.cgiar.org/Publications/Annual Report/2000/Project%204.2%20B/Project4.2B.html> (February 1, 2005).

3. Mohammed Marmaduke Pickthall, trans., Qur'an, chapter 3, verses 31 and 32, *The Meaning of The Glorious Koran* (New York: New American Library, n.d.), p. 83.

4. Kristine Uhlman, "Overview Of Shari'a and Prevalent Customs In Islamic Societies—Divorce and Child Custody," *Family Law, Expert Law, The Law Offices of Aaron Larson,* January 2004, <http://www.expertlaw.com/library/ family _law/islamic_custody-2.html#54> (June 15, 2005).

5. Lee Smith, "Mideast Meets West—Syrian Youth Embrace American Culture," *TravelandLeisure.com,* November 2005, <http://www.travelandleisure.com /invoke.cfm?ObjectID=EFC1B056-B7D7-4544 -824754C558F8F957> (October 22, 2005).

6. Center for Monitoring the Impact of Peace, *CMIP Reports,* June 2001, <http://www.edume.org/reports/6/1 .htm> (October 22, 2005).

Chapter 5. Early History

1. Afaf Sabeh McGowan, "Chapter 1: Historical Setting: Ancient Syria," *Syria: A Country Study,* Thomas Collelo, ed. (Washington: GPO for the Library of Congress, 1988), pp. 7–8.

2. Daniel W. Brown, *A New Introduction to Islam* (Oxford: Blackwell Publishing, 2004), p. 8, <http://www. blackwellpublishing.com/content/BPL_Images/Content _store/Sample_chapter/0631216030/Brown-001.pdf> (June 22, 2005).

3. Sue M. Sefscik, "Zenobia," *Women's History, About.com,* n.d., <http://womenshistory.about.com/library/bio/ucbio_zenobia.htm> (June 22, 2005).

4. Steve Muhlberger, "The Arabs as Conquerors," *History 2805—History of Islamic Civilization, Nipissing University,* Ontario, Canada, March 13, 2004, <http://www.nipissingu.ca/department/history/muhlberger/2805/conqors.htm> (June 22, 2005).

5. Quoted in Lynn Teo Simarski, "Visions of Damascus," *Aramco World,* Vol. 42, No. 2, March/April 1991, p. 25.

6. John L. Esposito, *Islam: The Straight Path* (New York: Oxford University Press, 1988), p. 64.

Chapter 6. Modern History

1. "Greater Syria," Cedarland, n.d., <http://www.cedarland.org/syria.html> (June 26, 2005).

2. Afaf Sabeh McGowan, "Chapter 1: Historical Setting: World War I and Arab Nationalism," *Syria: A Country Study,* Thomas Collelo, ed. (Washington: GPO for the Library of Congress, 1988), p. 20.

3. Afaf Sabeh McGowan, "Chapter 1: Historical Setting: The Assad Era," *Syria: A Country Study,* Thomas Collelo, ed. (Washington: GPO for the Library of Congress, 1988), p. 44.

Chapter 7. Economy

1. Steven Plaut, "The Collapsing Syrian Economy," *The Middle East Quarterly,* Vol. VI, No. 3, September 1999, <http://www.meforum.org/article/476> (October 22, 2005).

2. Info-Prod Research (Middle East), "Syria," *Country Studies,* n.d., <http://www.infoprod.co.il/article/25> (October 22, 2005).

3. Steven Plaut, "The Collapsing Syrian Economy," *The Middle East Quarterly.*

4. Rhonda E. Boris, "Chapter 3: The Economy, Agriculture: Land Reform," *Syria: A Country Study,* Thomas Collelo, ed. (Washington: GPO for the Library of Congress, 1988), p. 137.

5. Defense Language Institute: Foreign Language Center, Curriculum Development Division, Instructional Design Department, The Presidio of Monterey, California, *Syria in Perspective: An Orientation Guide,* p. 24, January 2004, <http://www.lingnet.org/areaStudies/perspectives/syria /syria.pdf> (October 14, 2005).

6. Alexander Sarris, "Agriculture in the Syrian Macroeconomic Context," *Syrian Agriculture at the Crossroads,* 2003, <http://www.fao.org /documents/show _cdr.asp?url_file=/DOCREP/006/Y4890E/y4890e05.htm> (July 1, 2005).

7. Faud N. Ghadry, "Syrian Reform: What Lies Beneath," *Middle East Quarterly,* Vol. XII, No. 1, Winter 2005, p. 65.

8. "Syria Mulls Limited Privatisation," *Aljazeera.Net,* June 7, 2005, <http://english.aljazeera.net/NR/exeres /9B17F323-BFB8-4074-A5D8-3BF4A446DD39.htm> (June 7, 2005).

Broyles, Matthew. *The Six-Day War*. New York: The Rosen Publishing Group, 2004.

Crompton, Samuel Willard. *The Third Crusade: Richard the Lionhearted vs. Saladin*. Philadelphia: Chelsea House Publishers, 2004.

Mir, Anjum. *The American Encounter with Islam*. Broomall, Pa.: Mason Crest Publishers, 2004.

Morrison, John. *Syria*. Philadelphia: Chelsea House Publishers, 2003.

Rosenberg, Aaron. *The Yom Kippur War*. New York: The Rosen Publishing Group, 2004.

Sears, Evelyn. *Muslims and the West*. Broomall, Pa.: Mason Crest Publishers, 2004.

Skinner, Patricia. *Syria*. Milwaukee: Gareth Stevens Publishing, 2004.

Stanley, Diane. *Saladin: Noble Prince of Islam*. New York: HarperCollins Publishers, 2002.

Whitehead, Kim. *Islam: The Basics*. Broomall, Pa.: Mason Crest Publishers, 2004.

The Middle East. Westport, Conn.: Greenwood Press, 2004.